A Drawing Mind Coloring Book: Color Me Free

Deborah Putnoi

ISBN-13: 978-1516847839

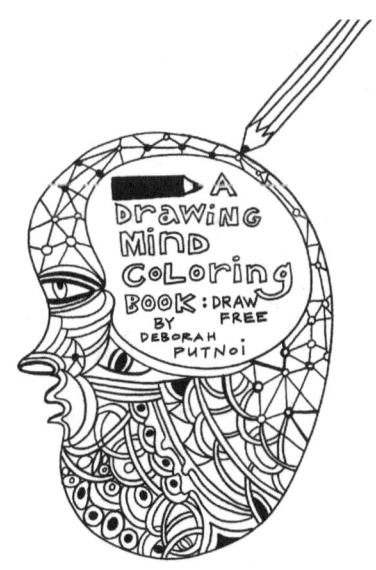

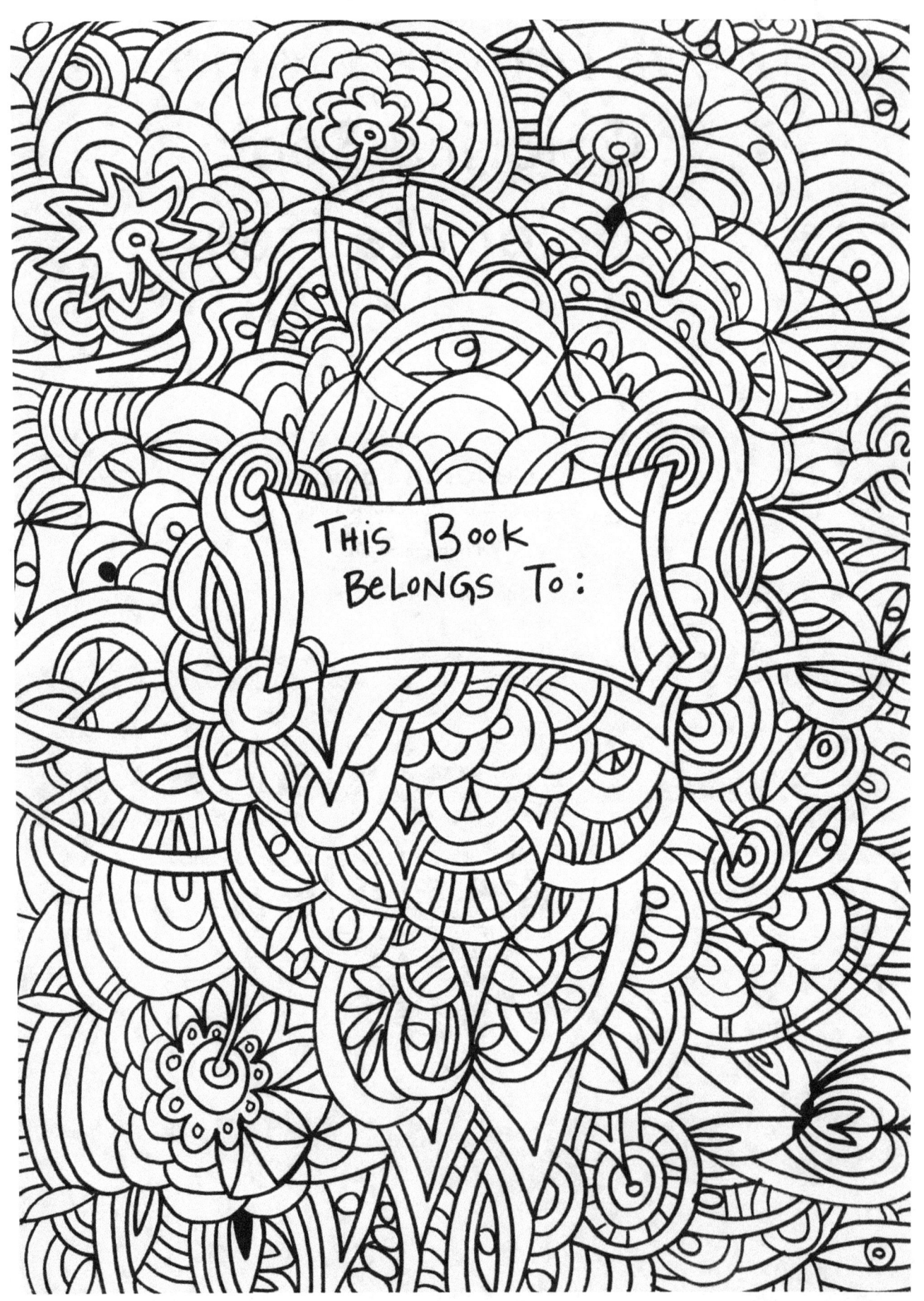

This Book Belongs To:

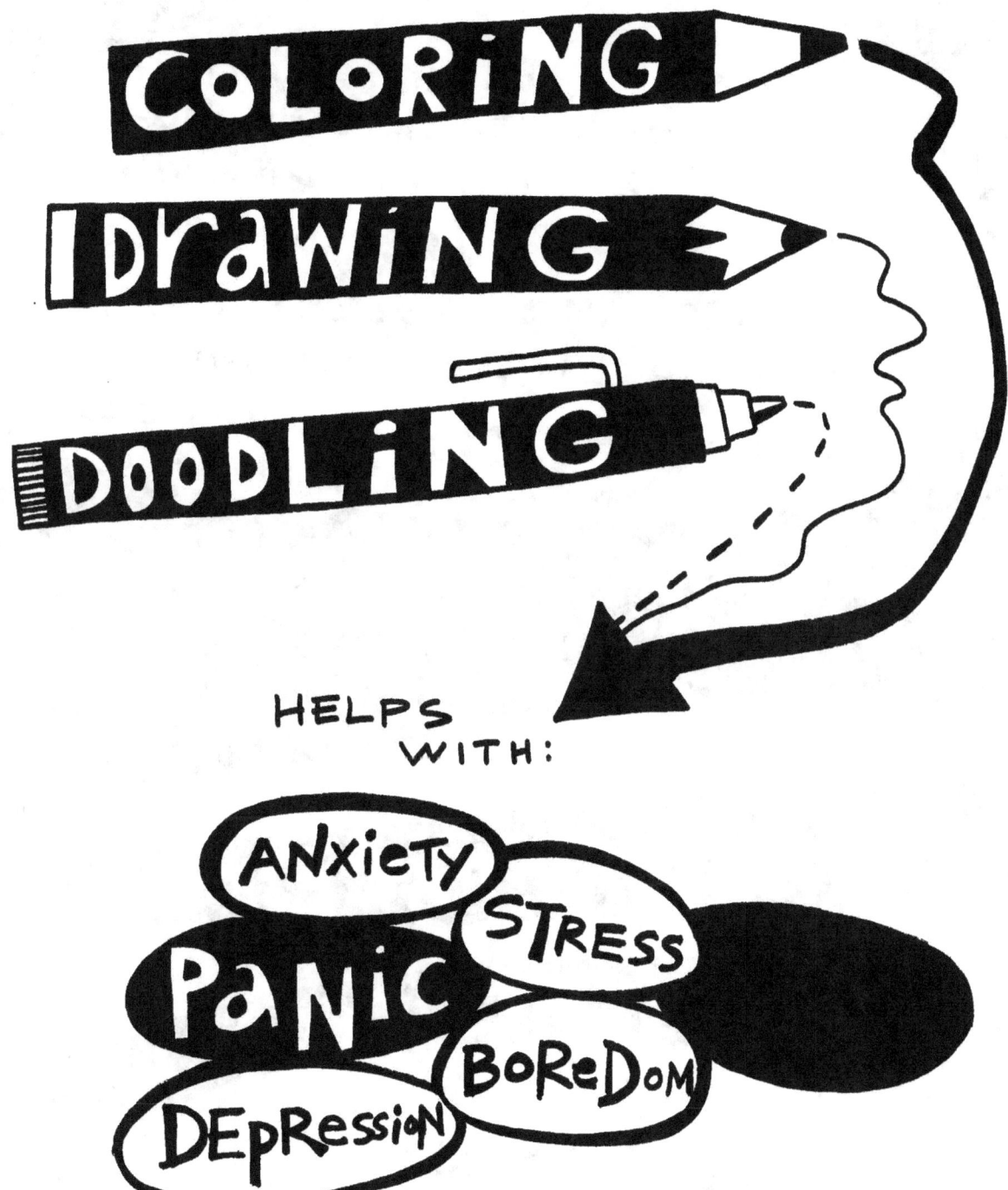

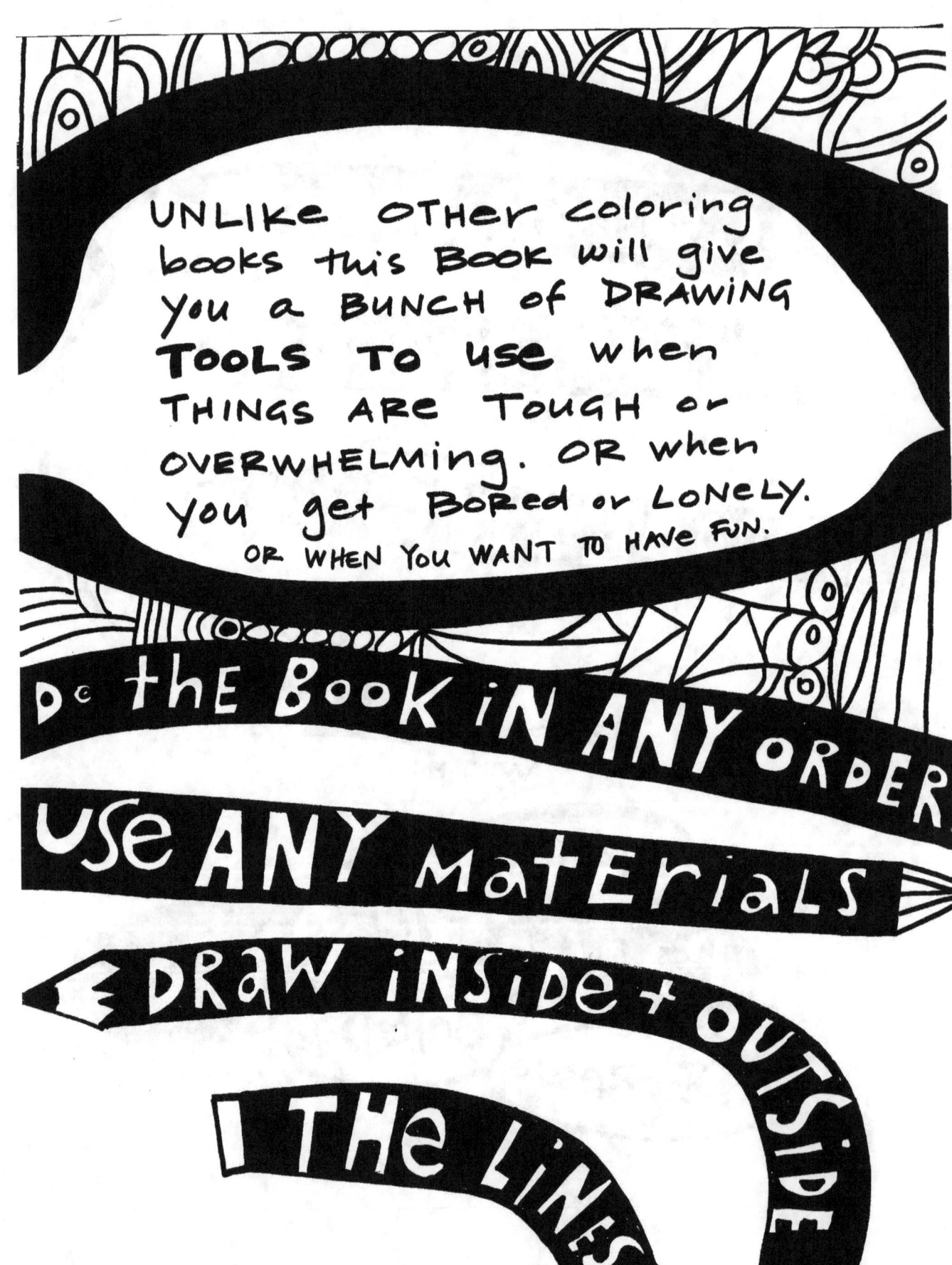

UNLIKE OTHer coloring books this BOOK will give You a BUNCH of DRAWING TOOLS TO use when THINGS ARE TOUGH or OVERWHELMing. OR when You get BOReD or LONELY. OR WHEN YOU WANT TO HAVE FUN.

Do the Book iN ANY oRDER

USE ANY maTErials

DRaW iNSiDe + OUTSiDE

THe LiNES

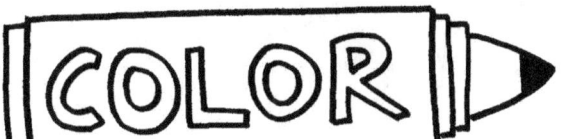

WHEN COLORING KEEP
THE COLOR WHEEL IN MIND

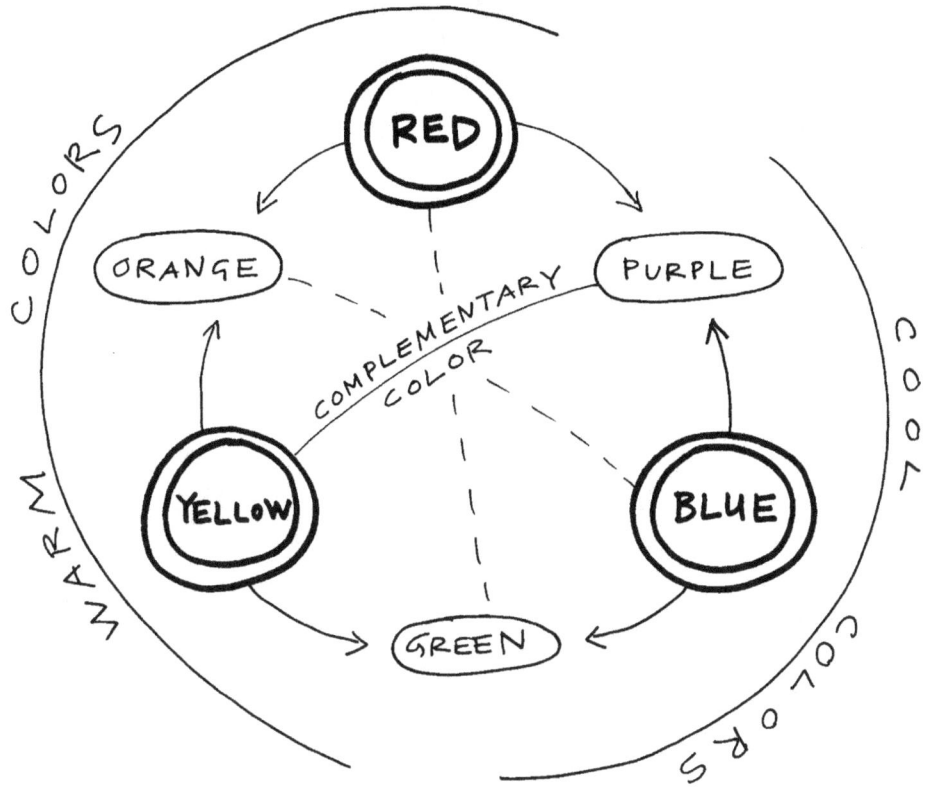

PRIMARY COLORS: RED, YELLOW, BLUE
You CAN'T MIX these COloRS

SECONDARY COLORS: ORANGE, PURPLE, GREEN
You CAN MIX these COLORS from
the primary colors.

COMPLEMENTARY COLORS: These colors sit
across from one another on the
color wheel. When placed next to
each other make a vibrant
contrast.

EXPERIMENT WITH COLOR!

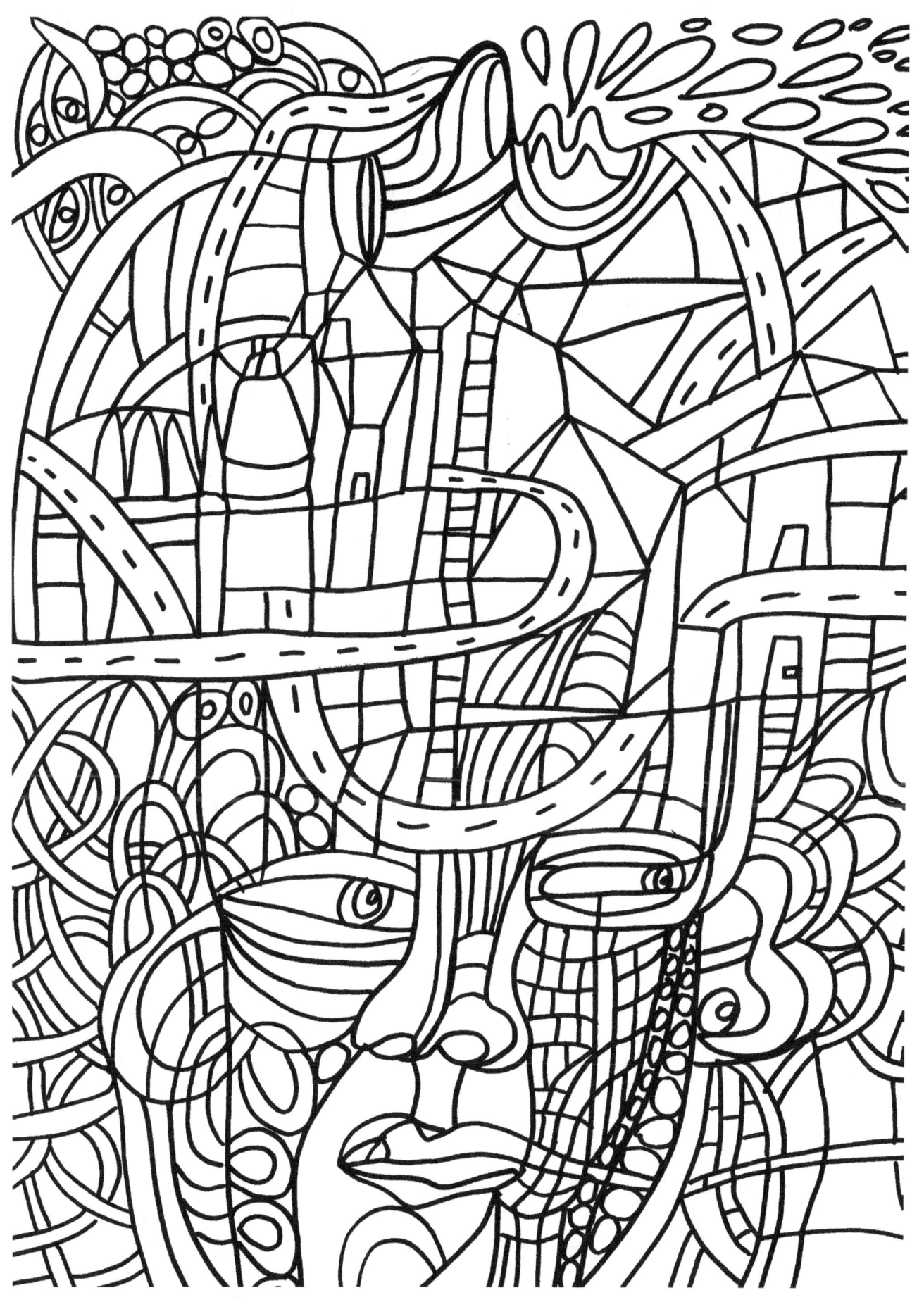

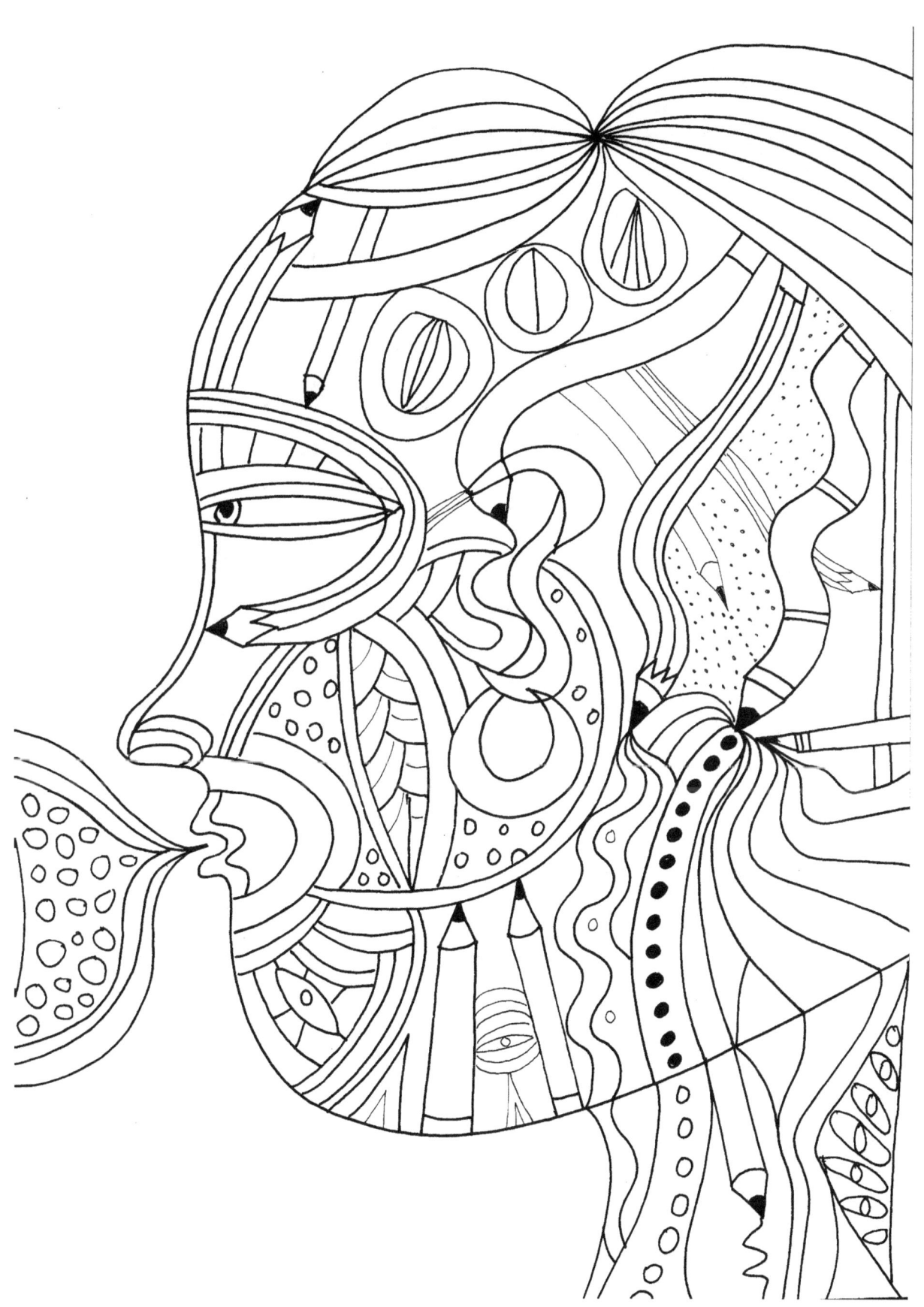

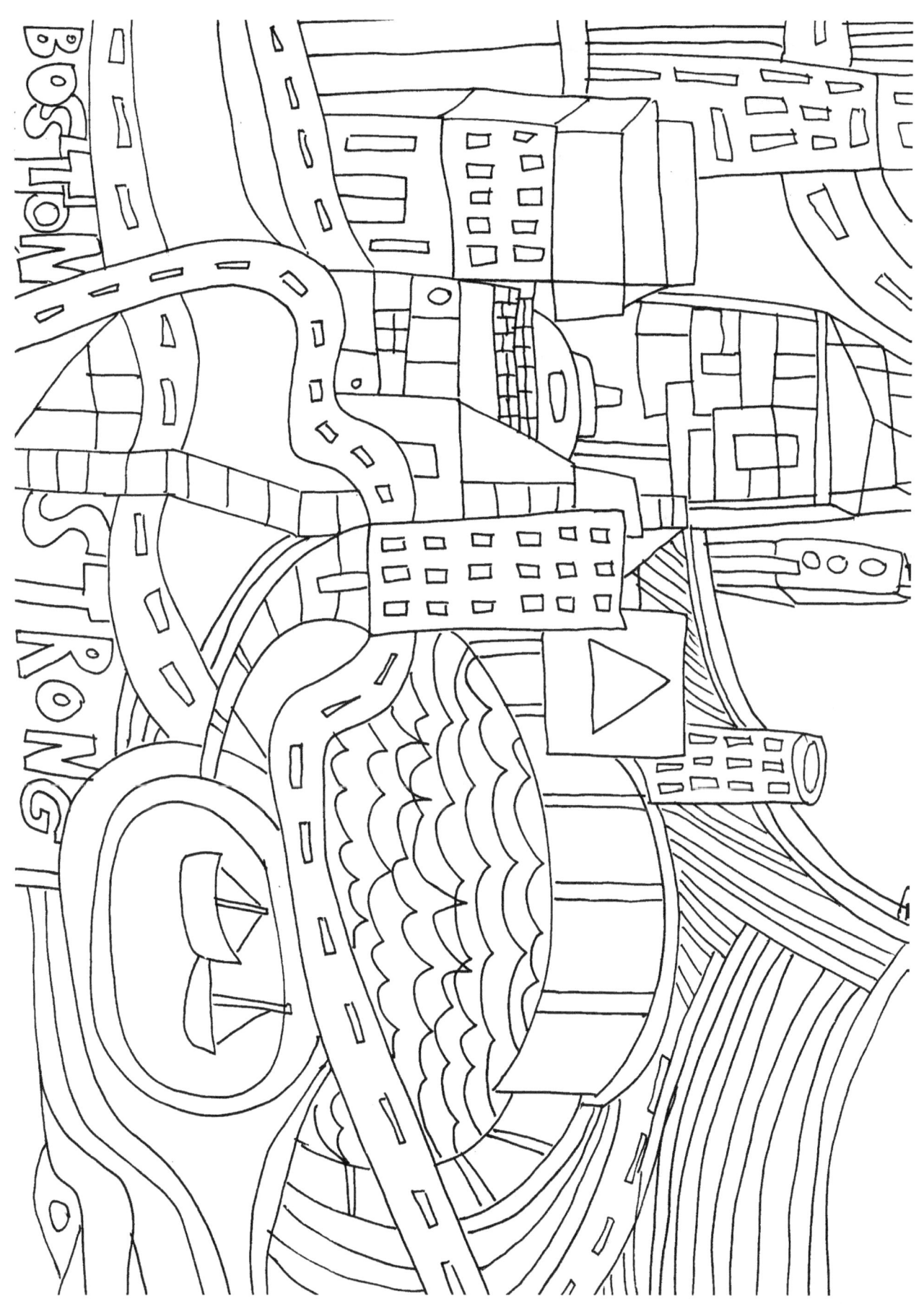

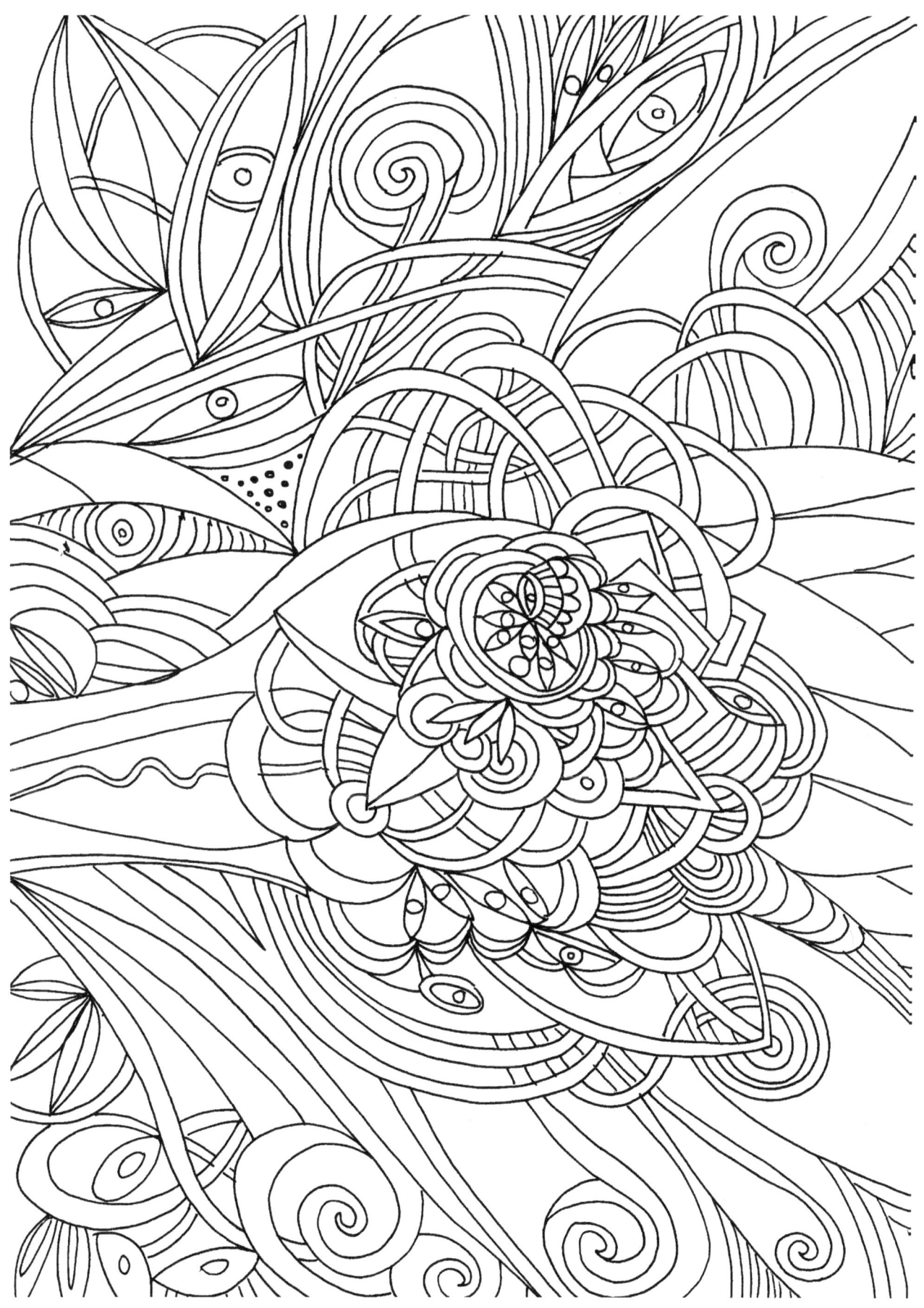

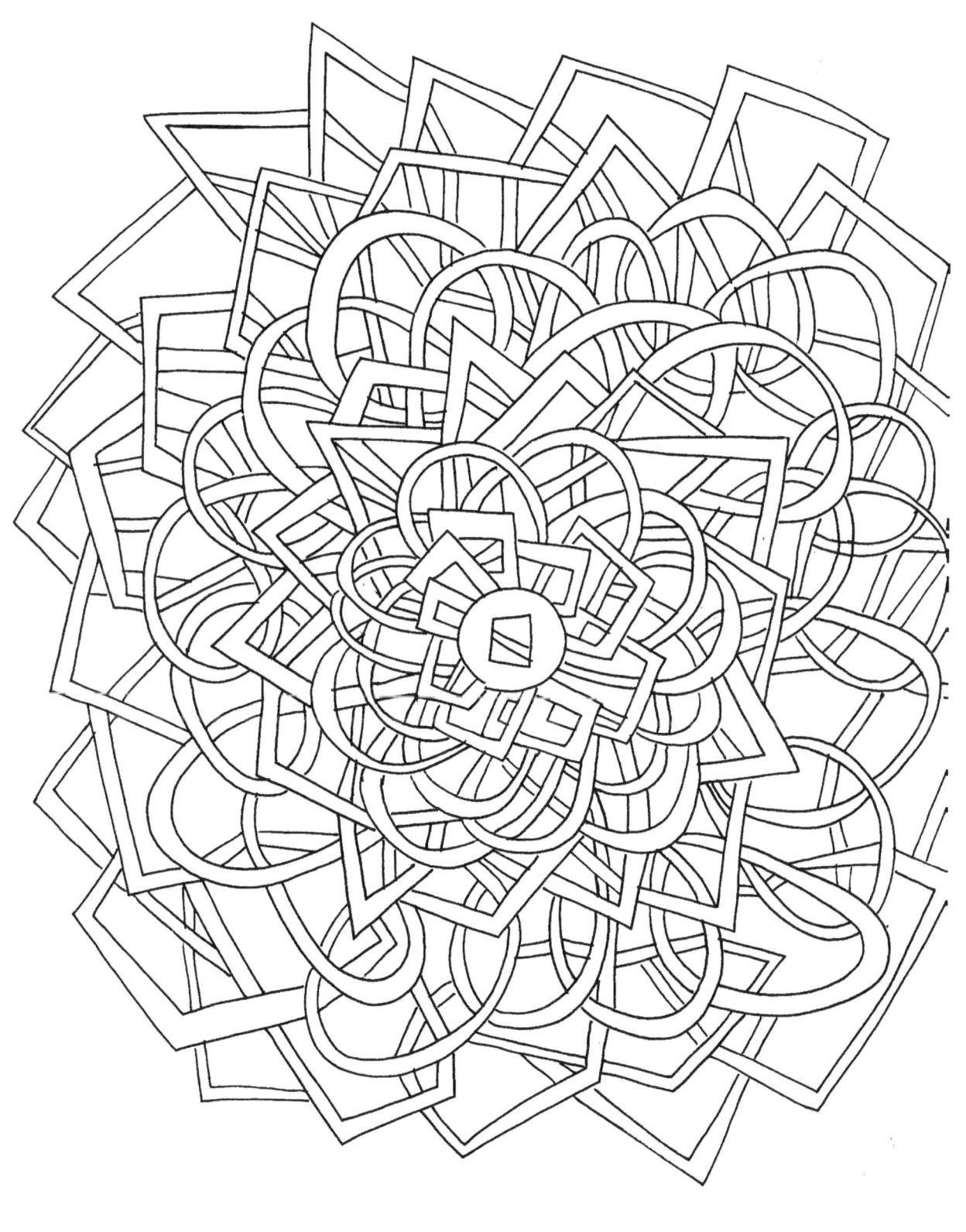

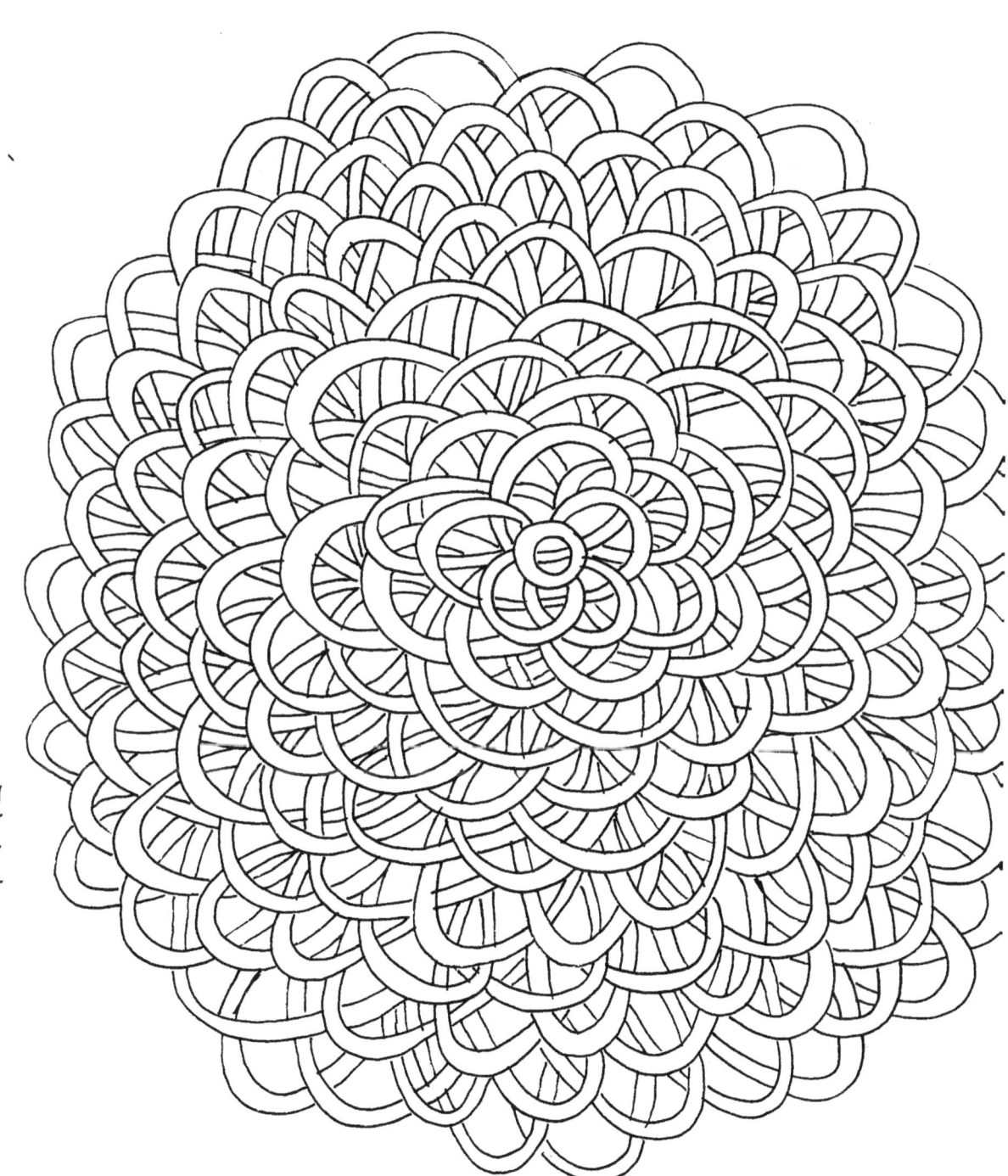

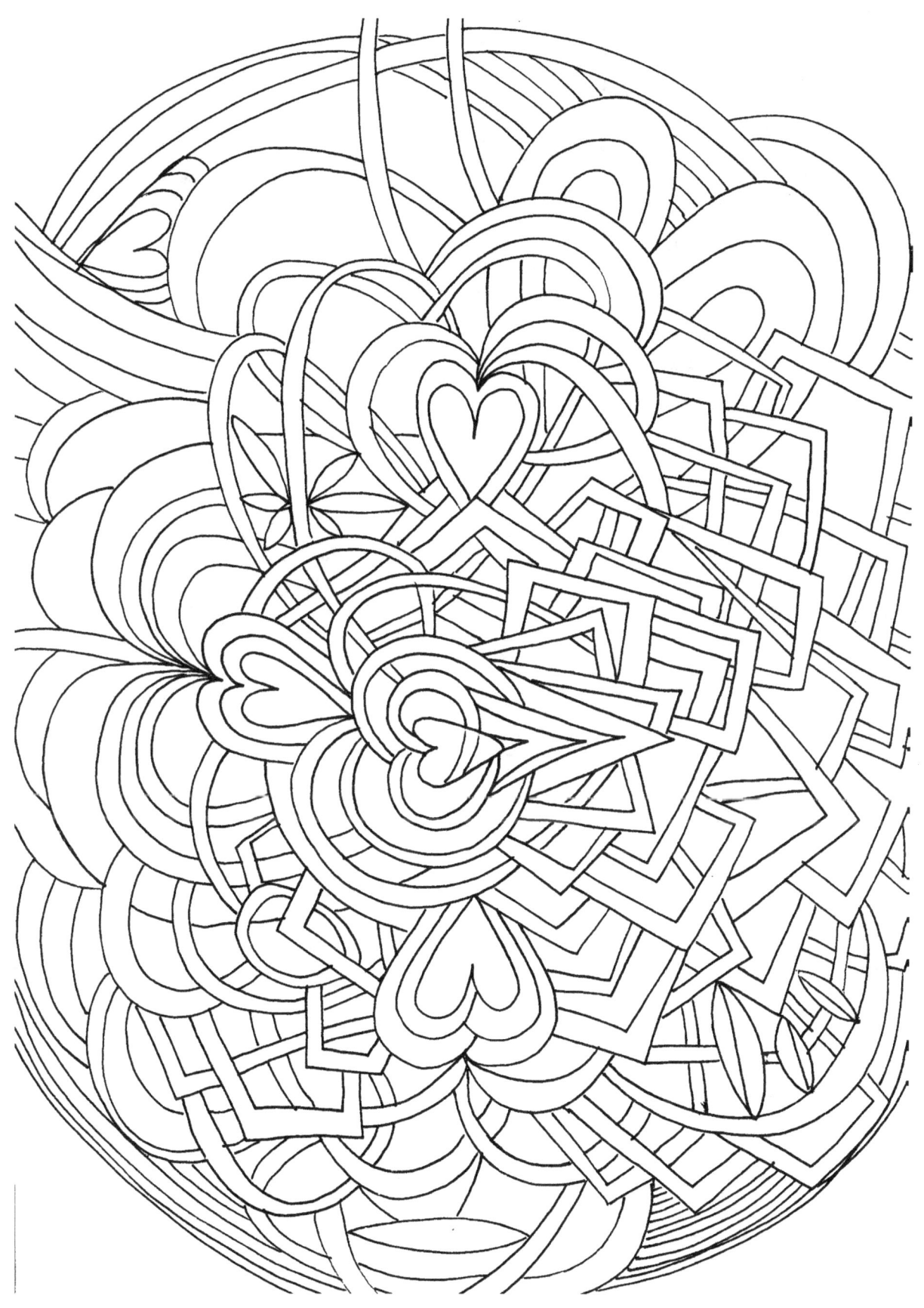

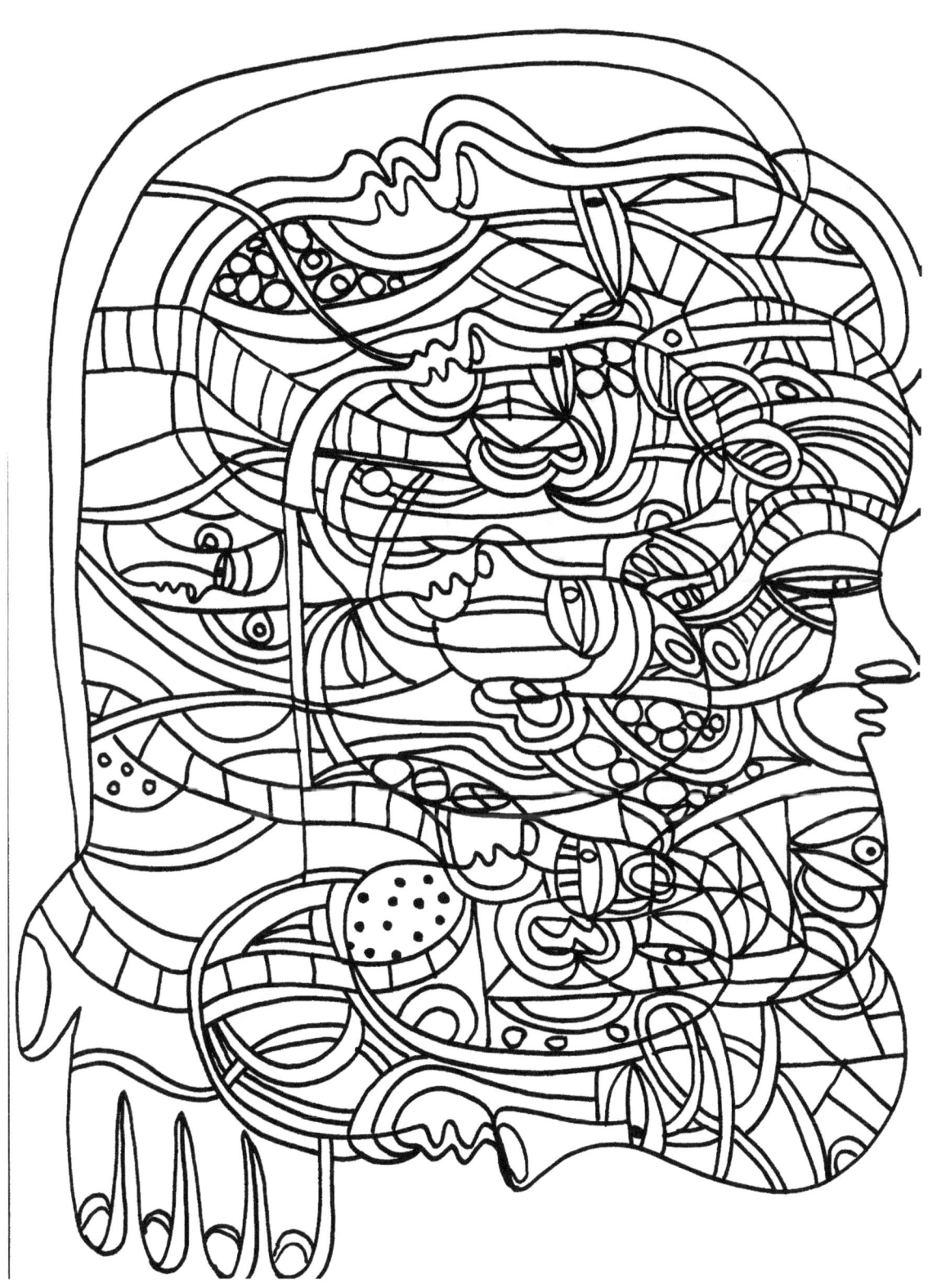

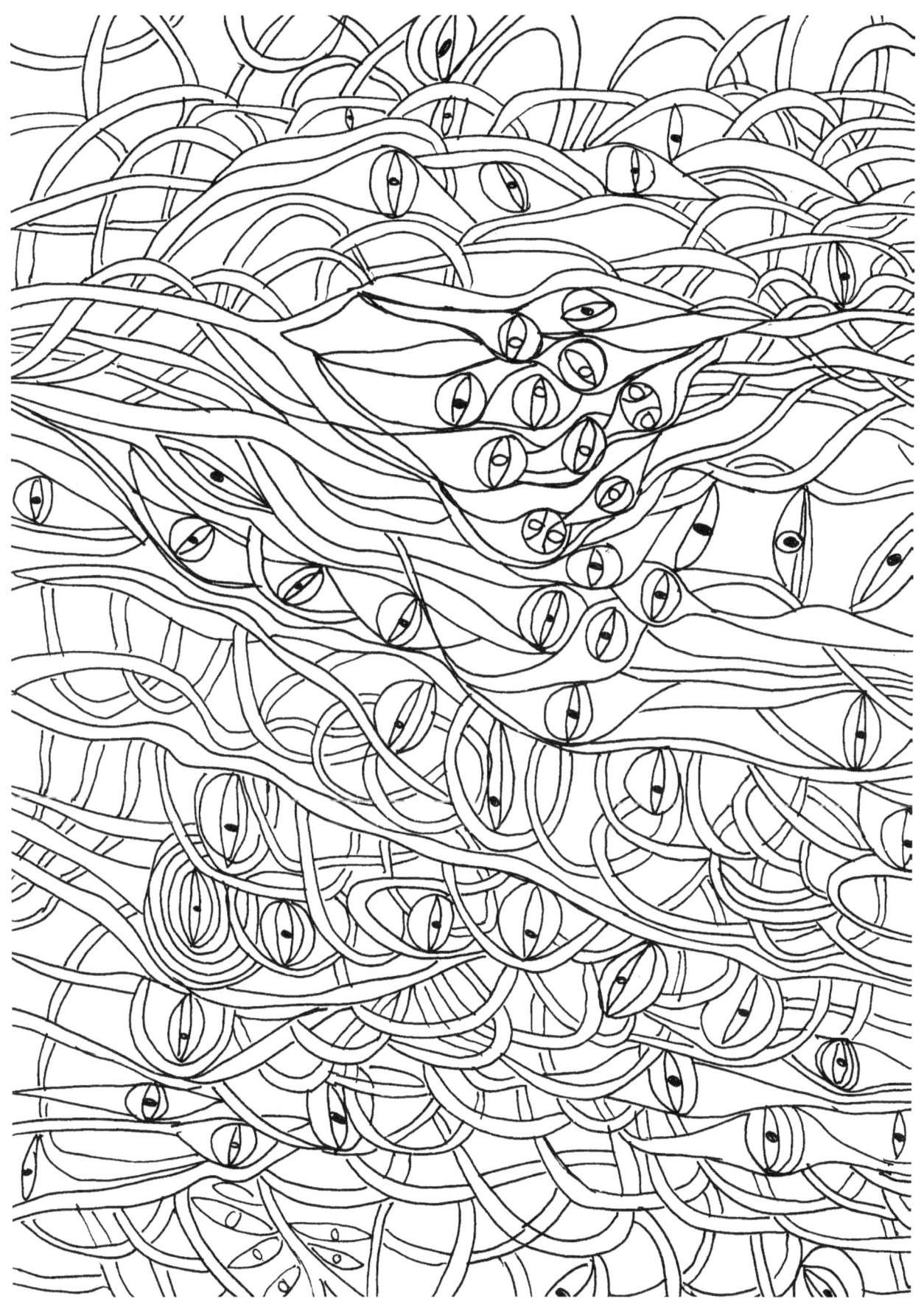

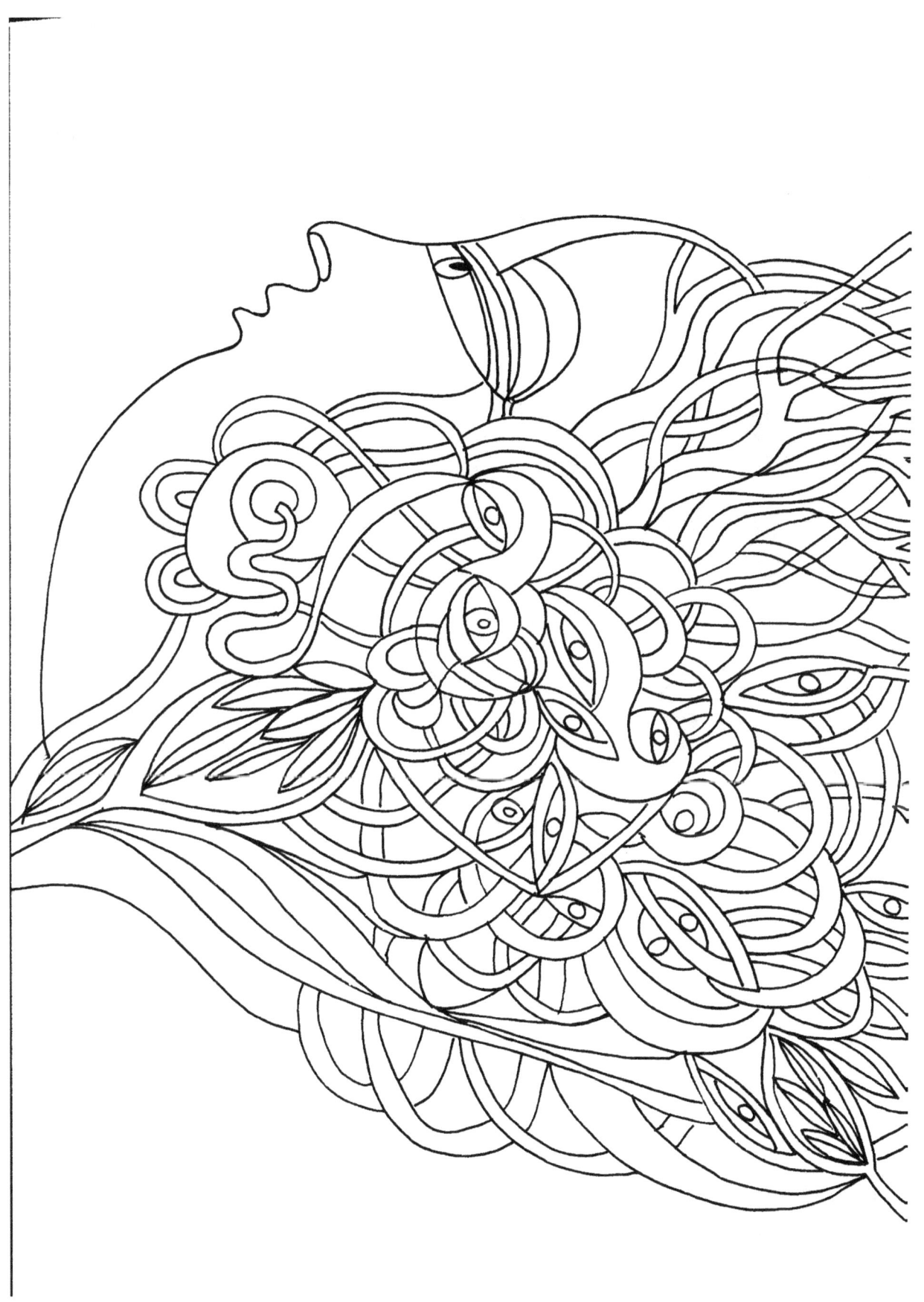

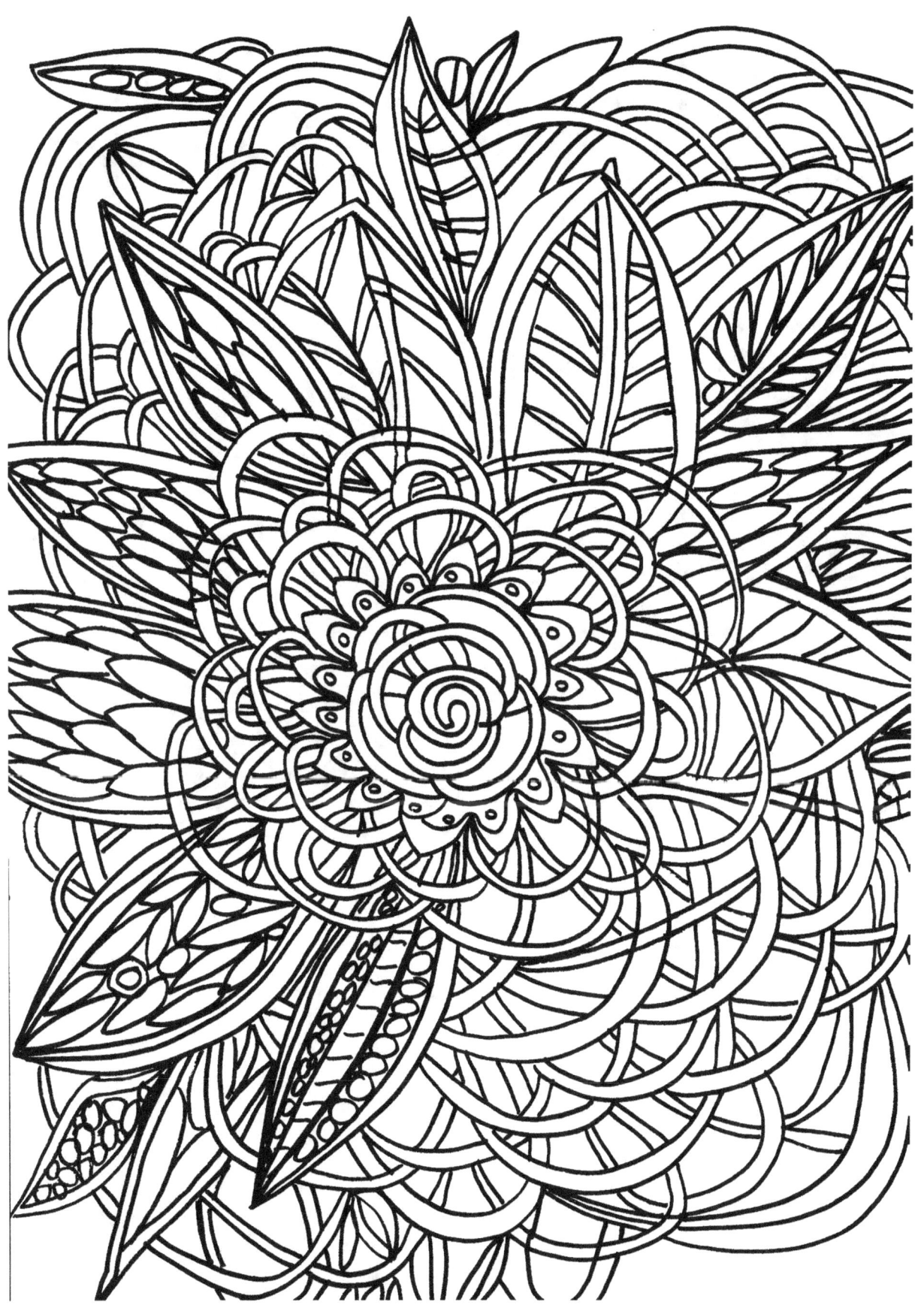

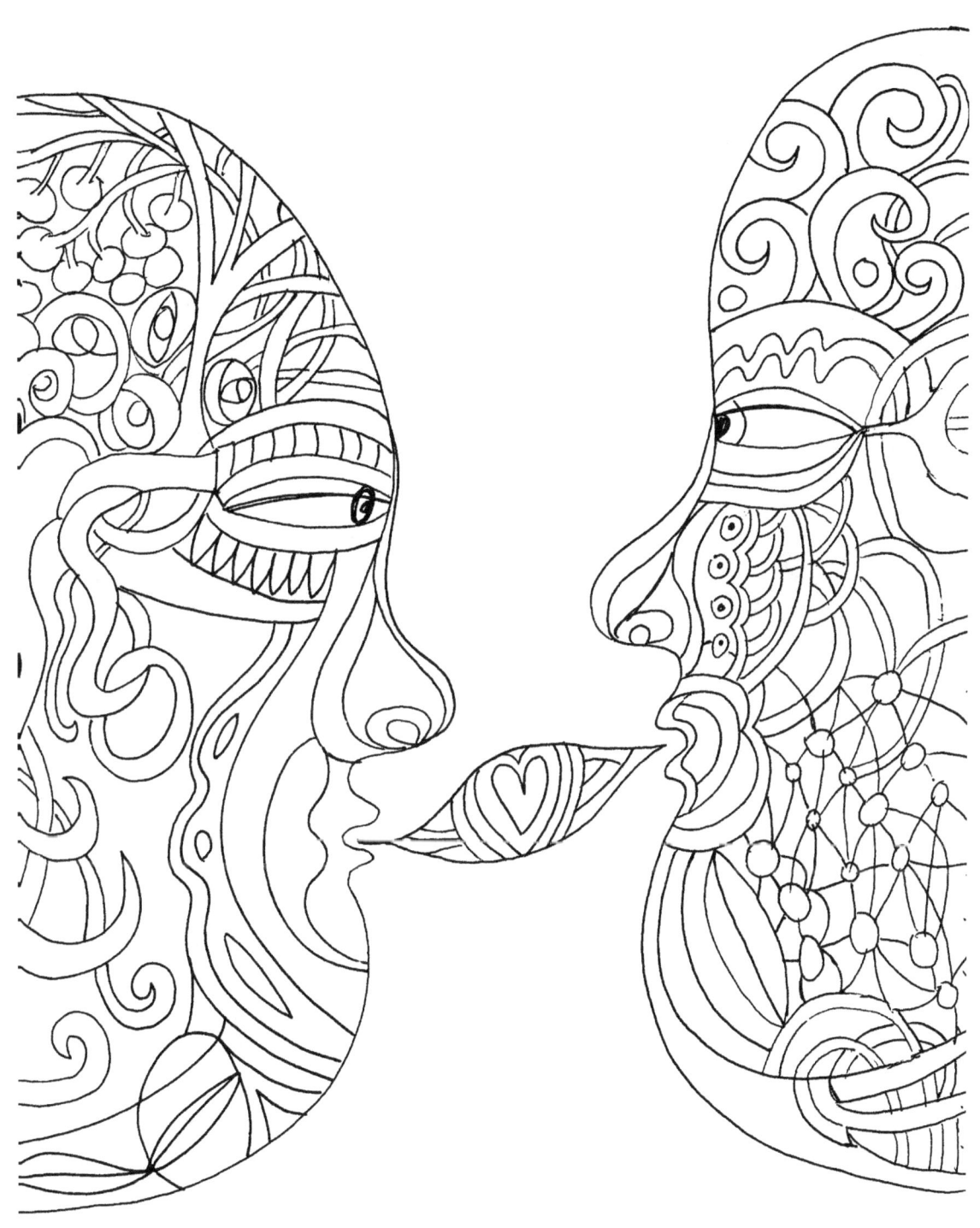

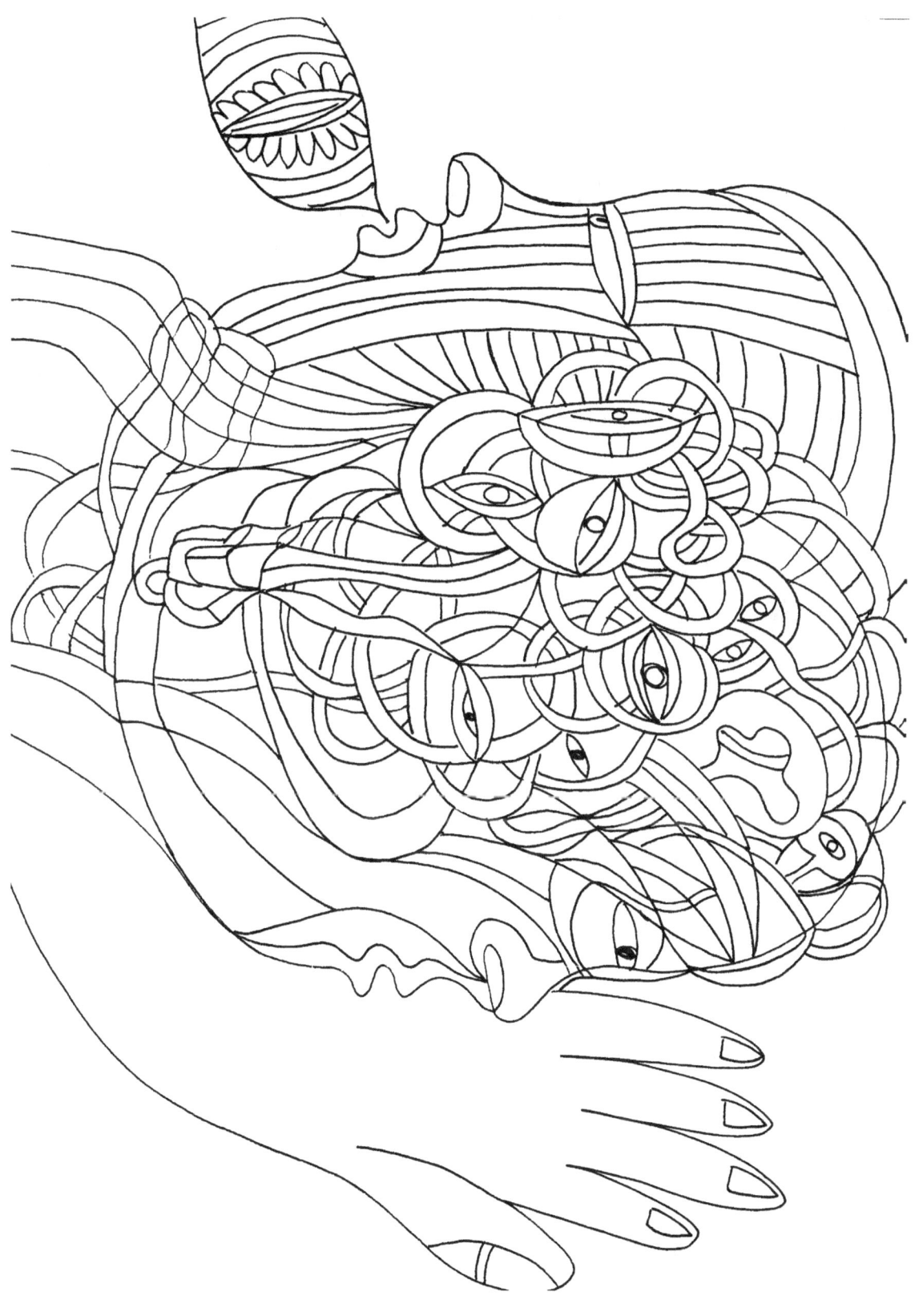

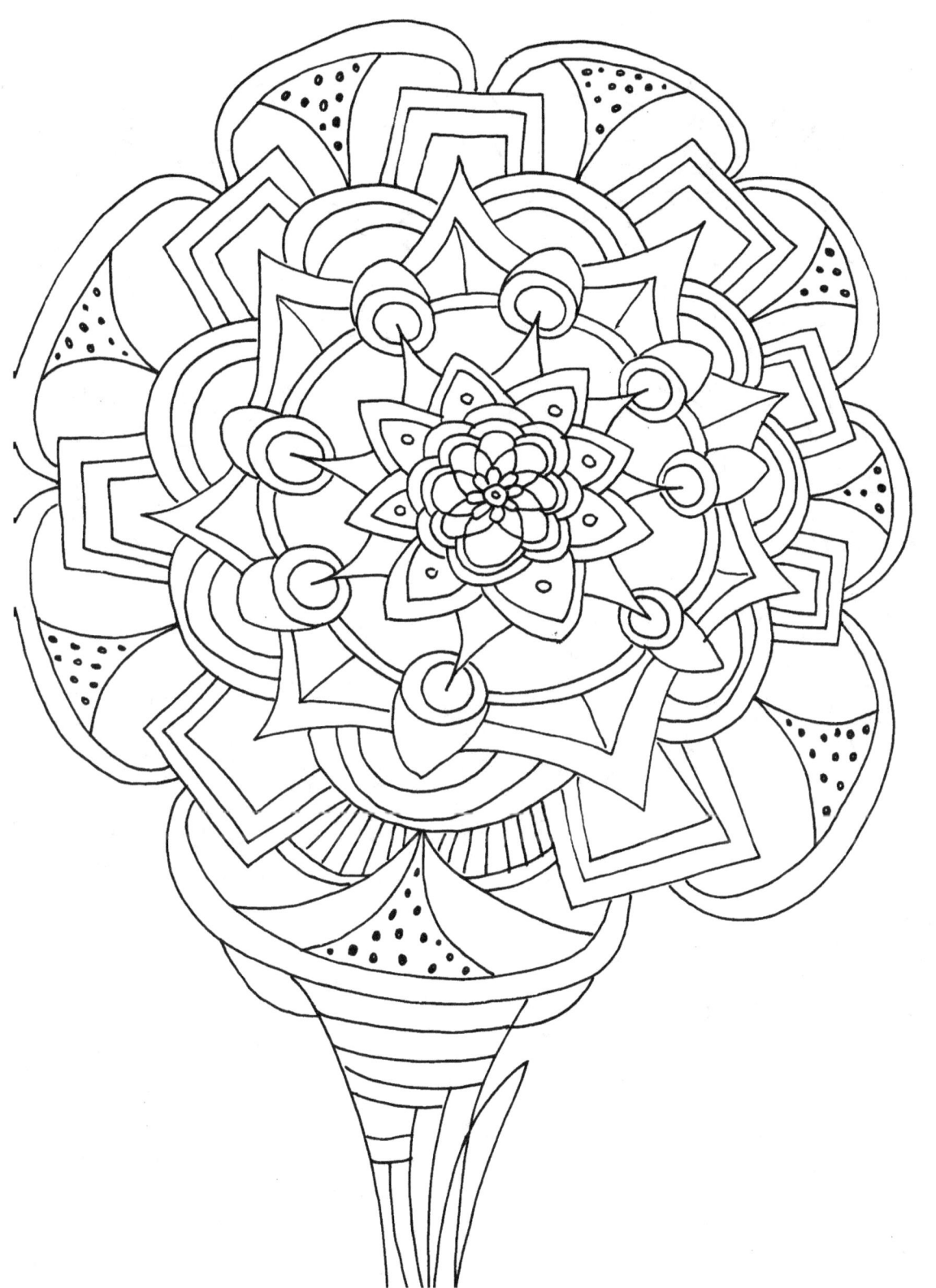

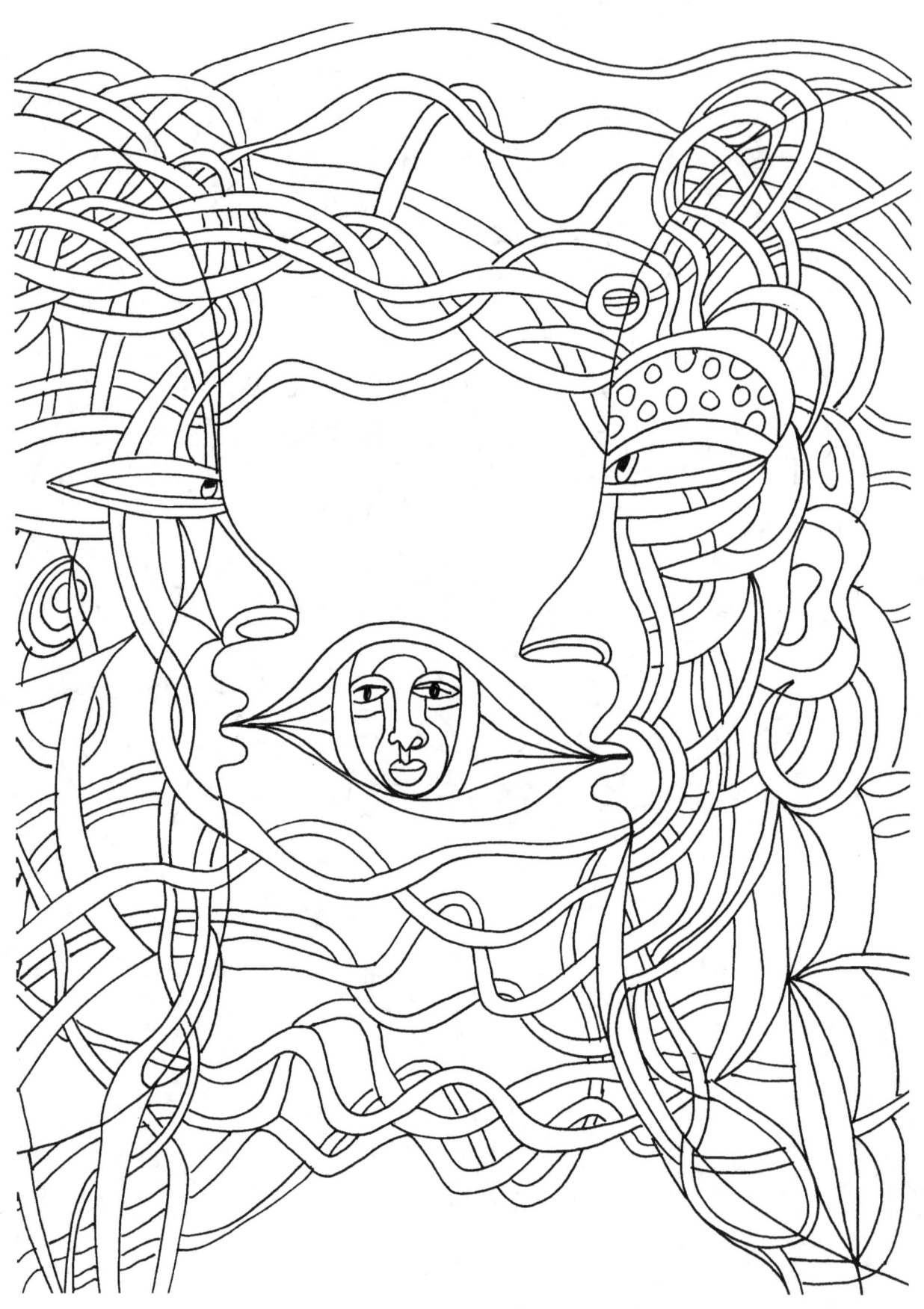

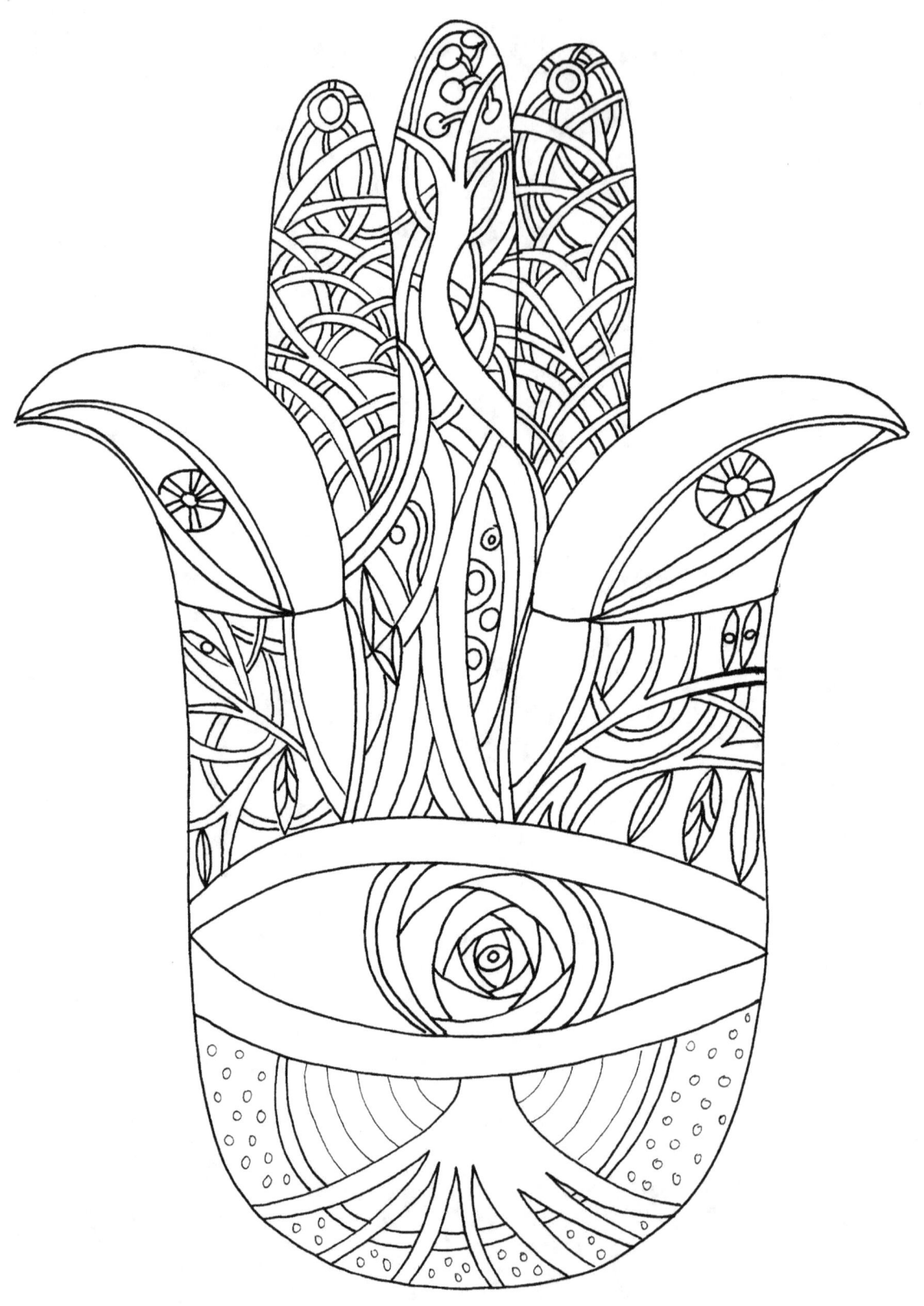

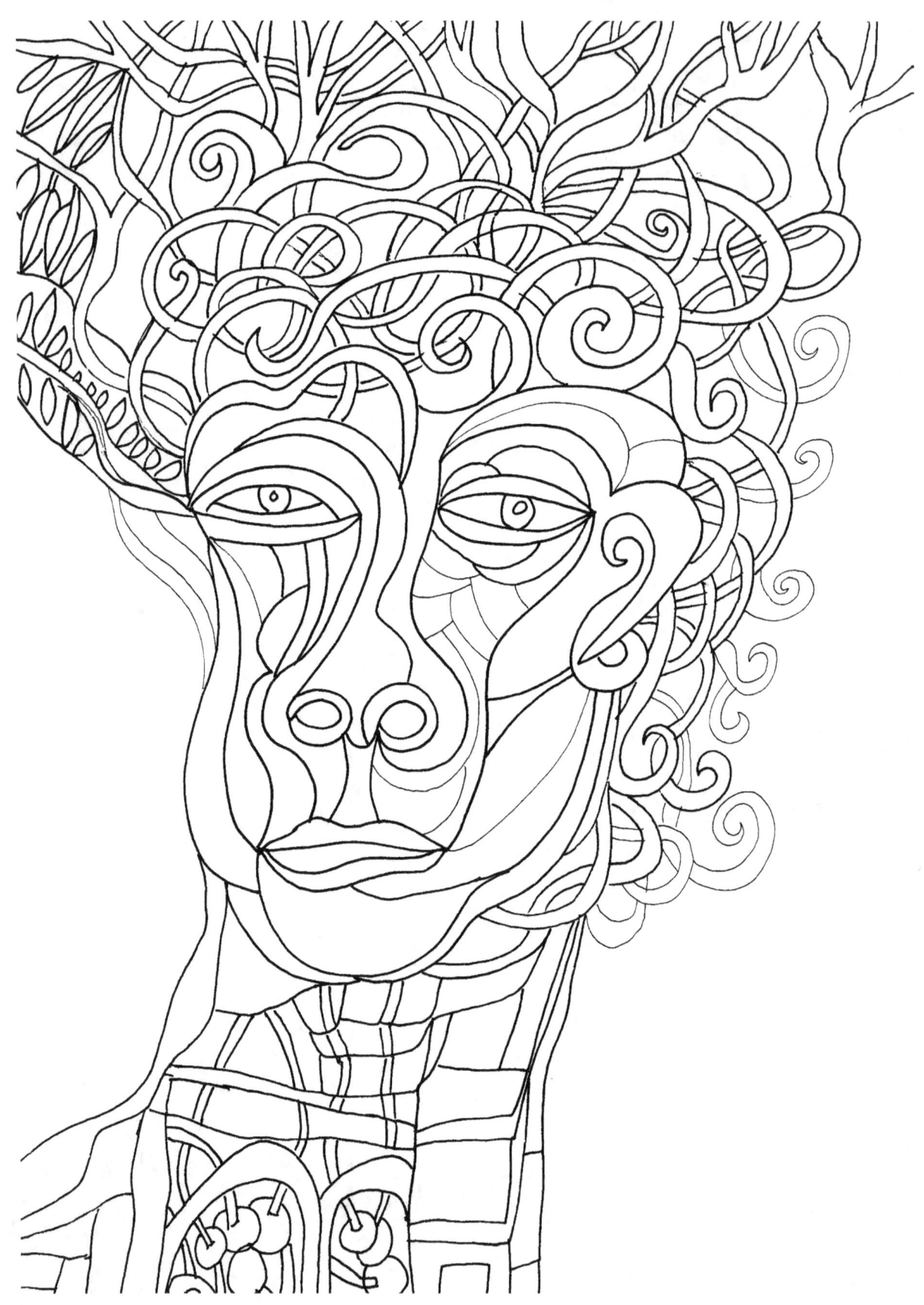

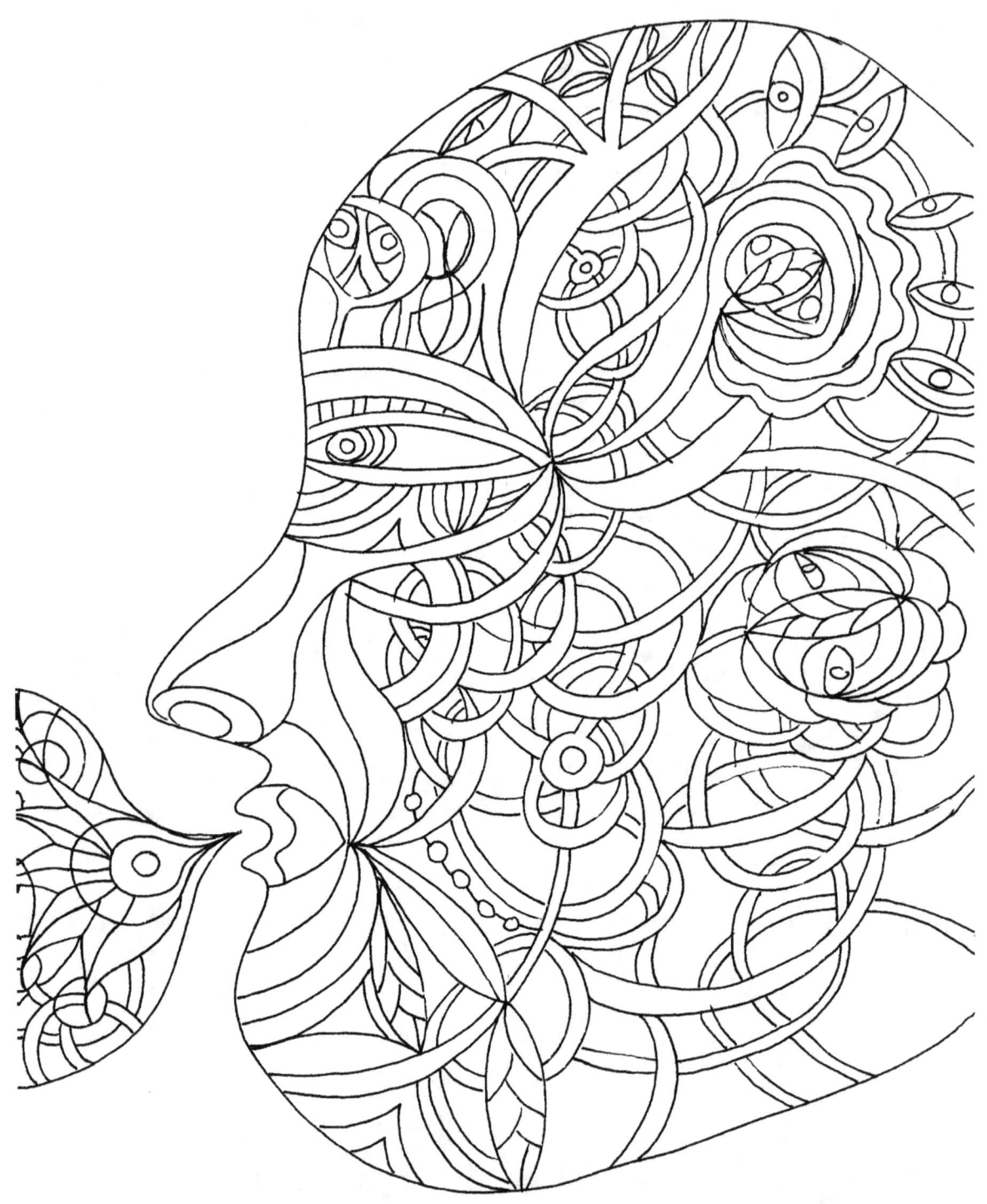

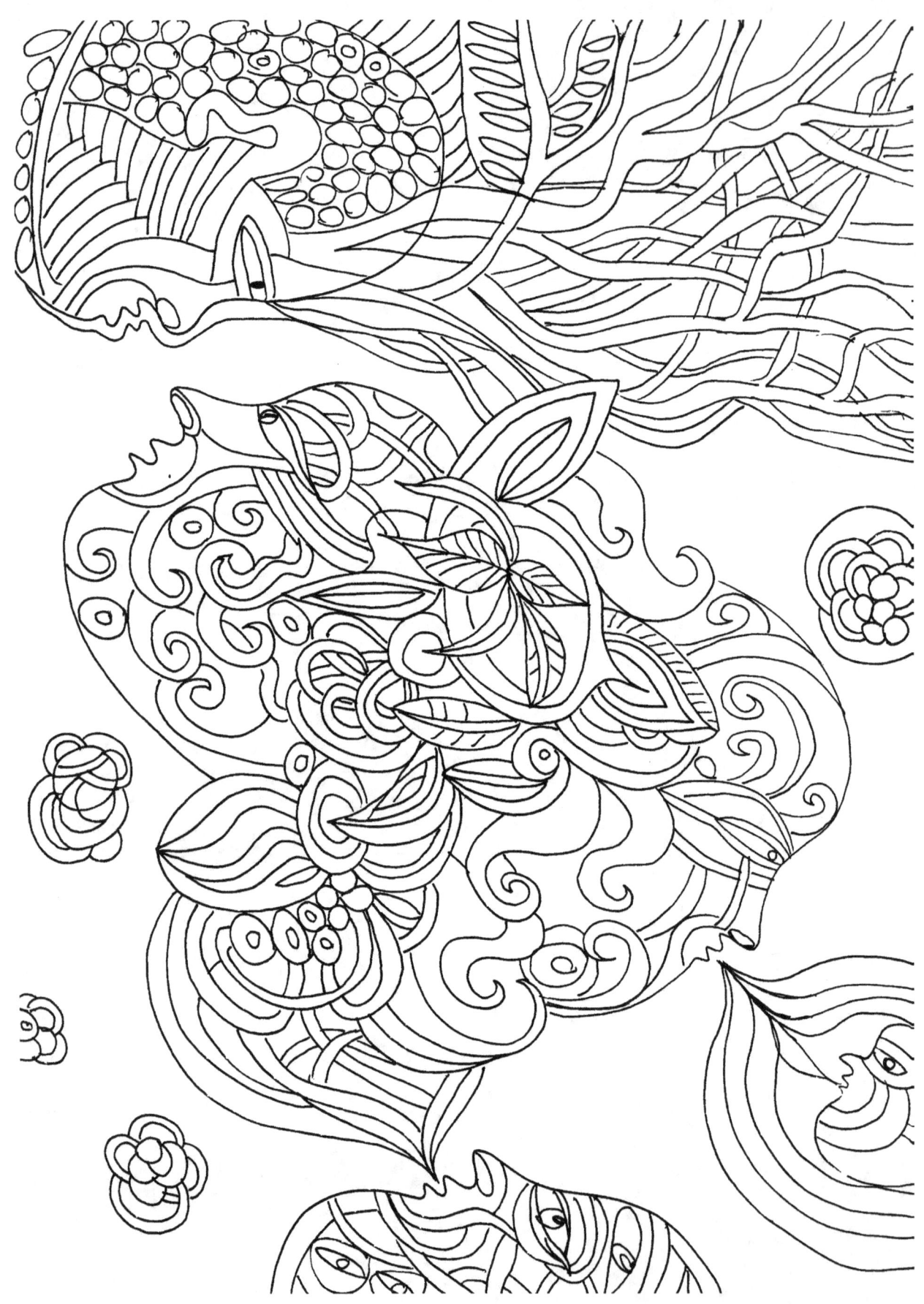

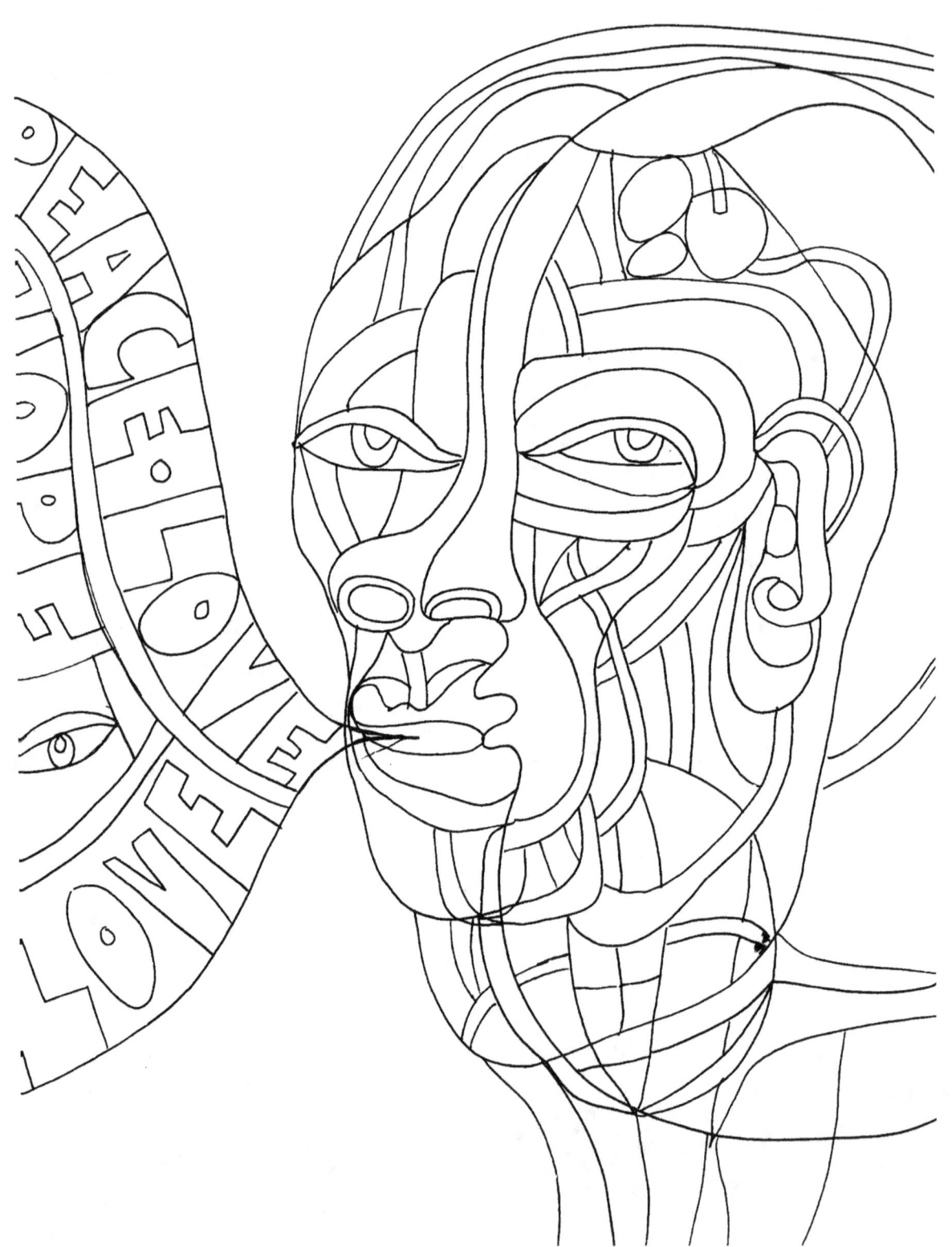

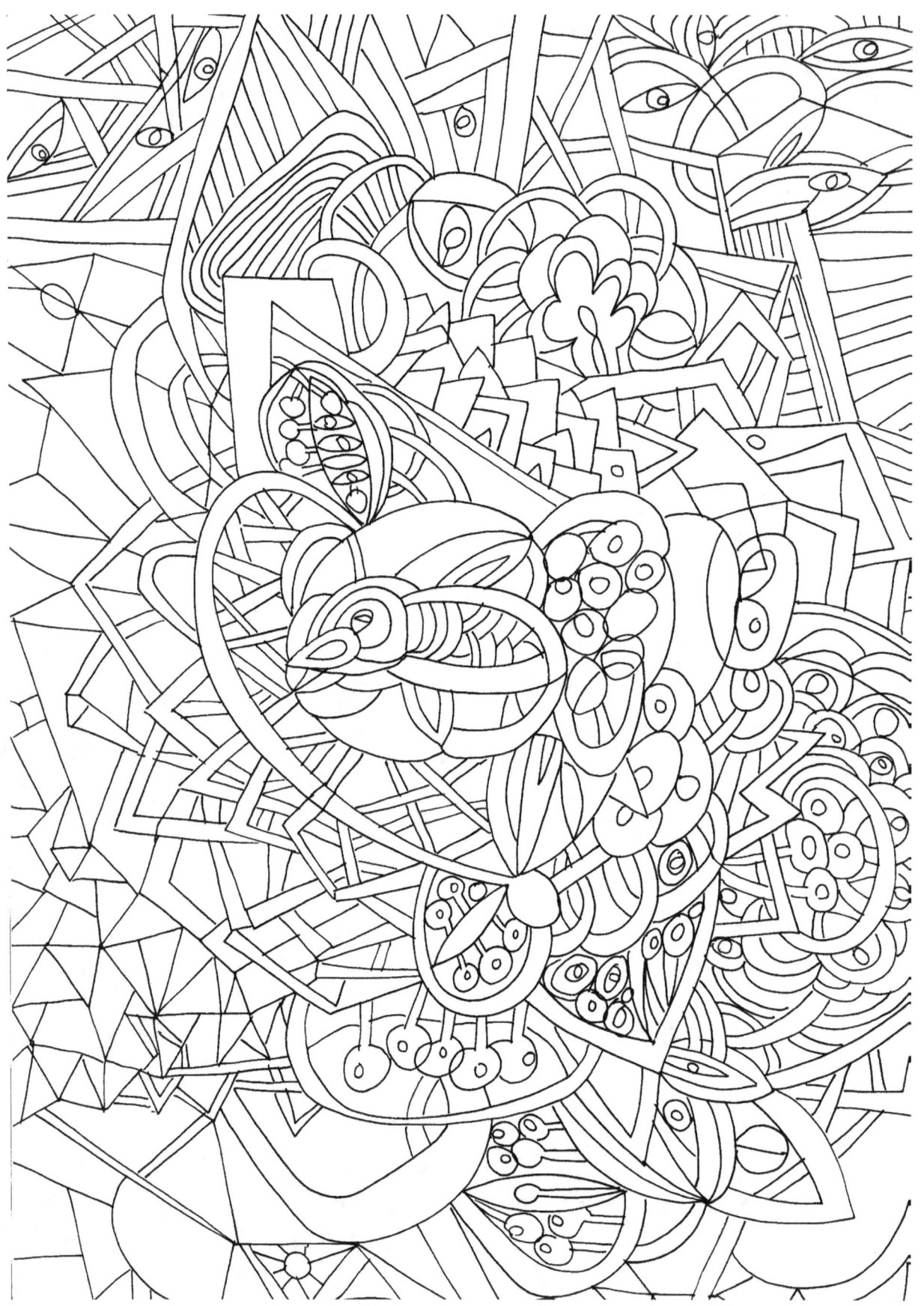

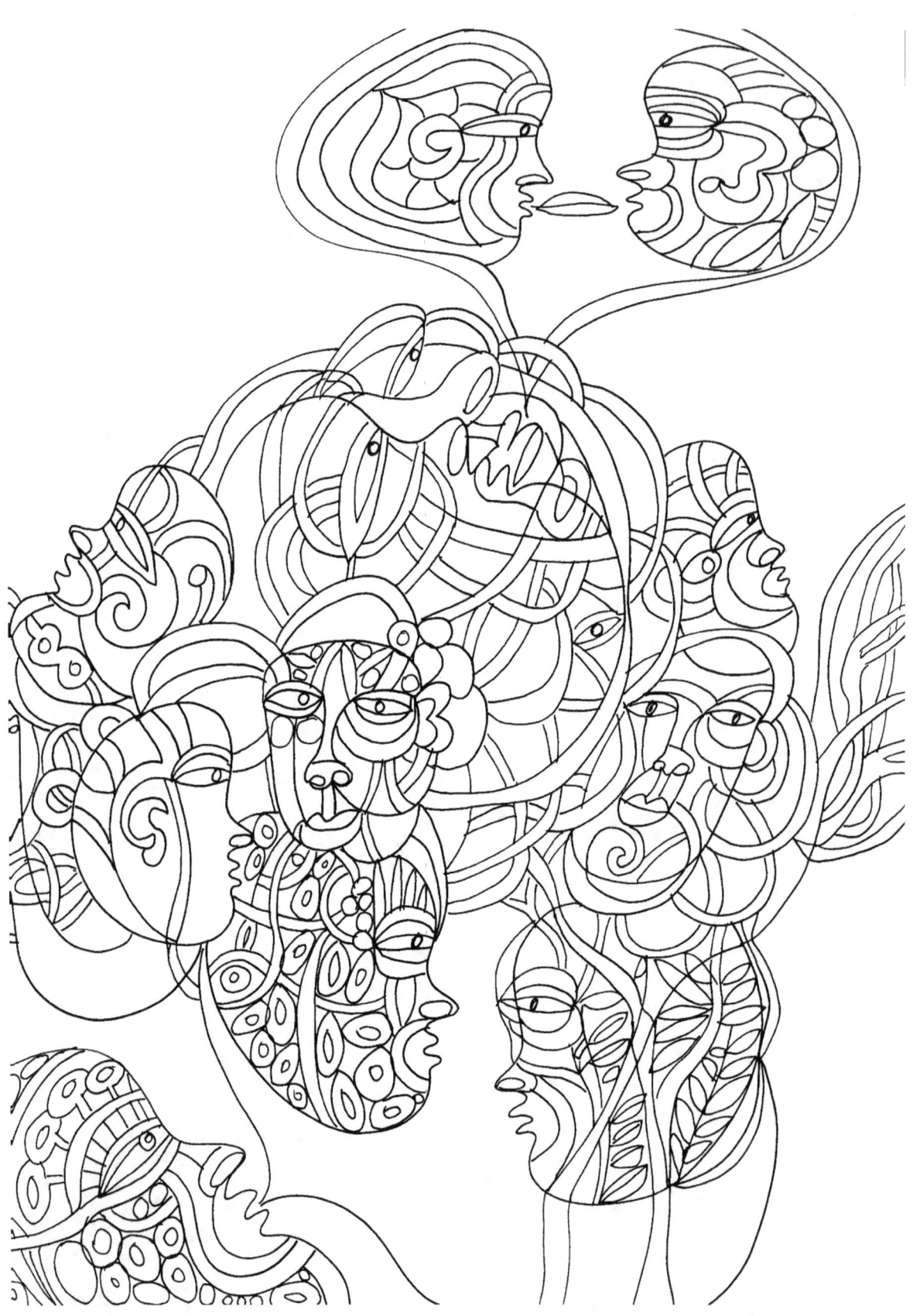

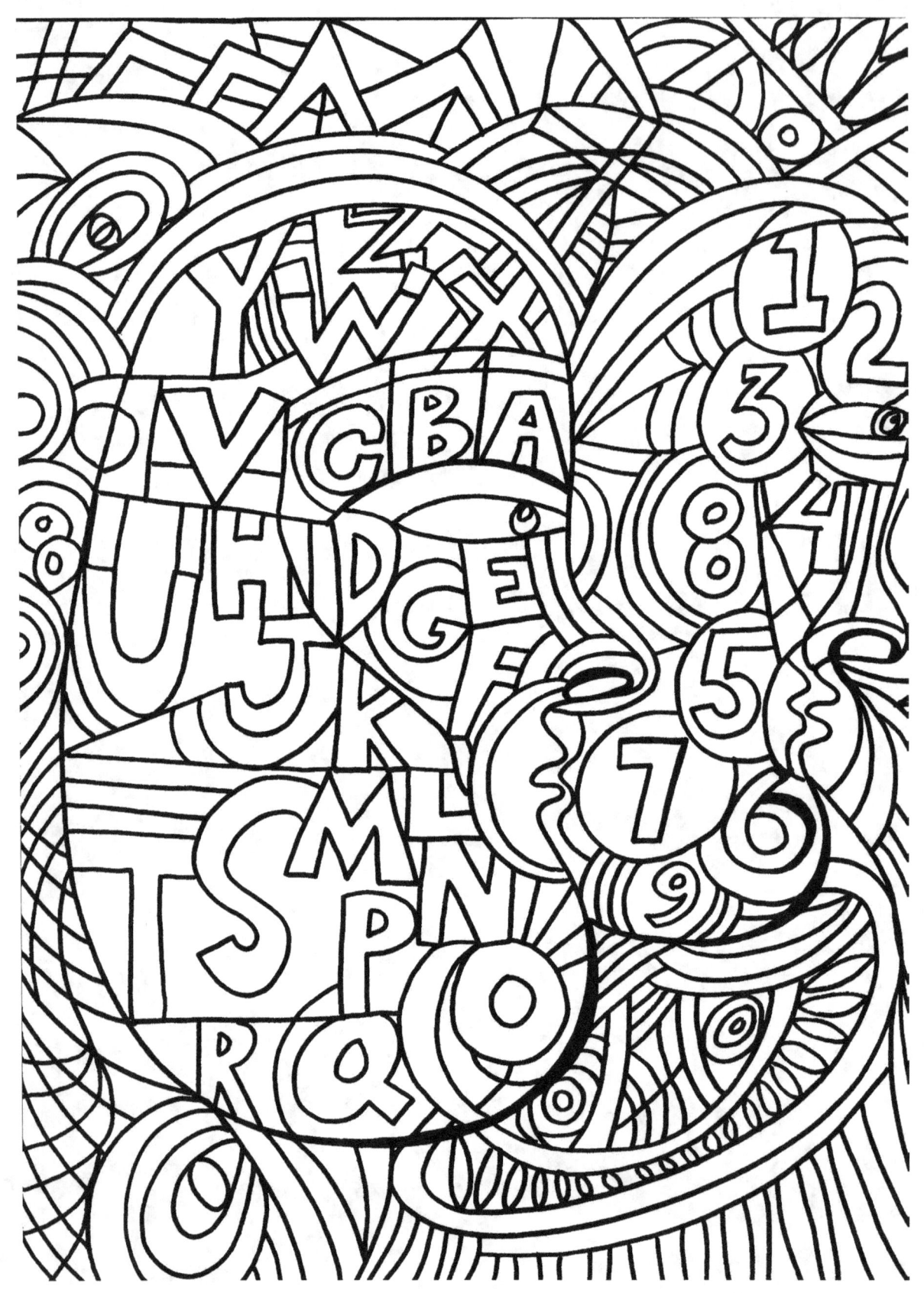

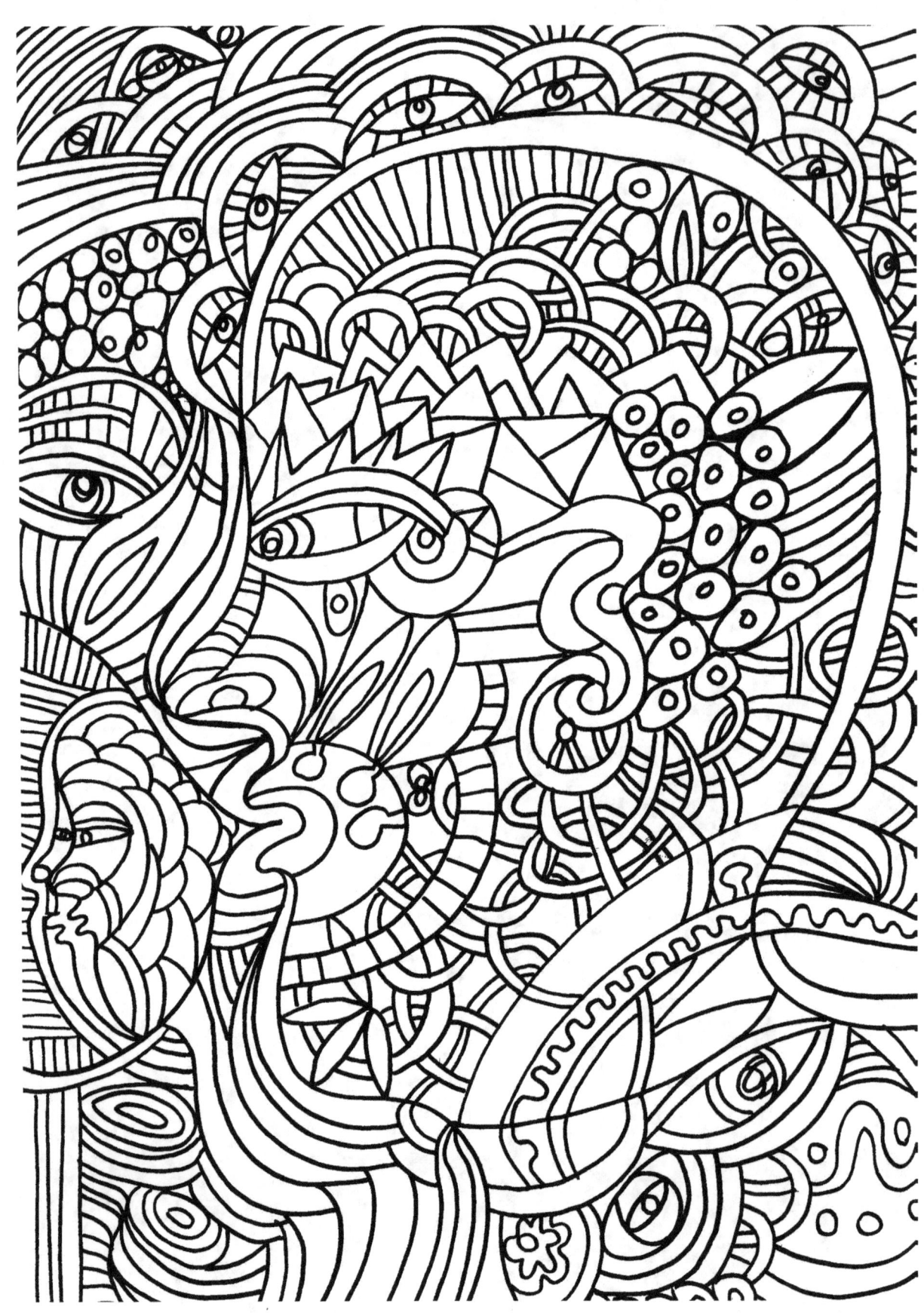

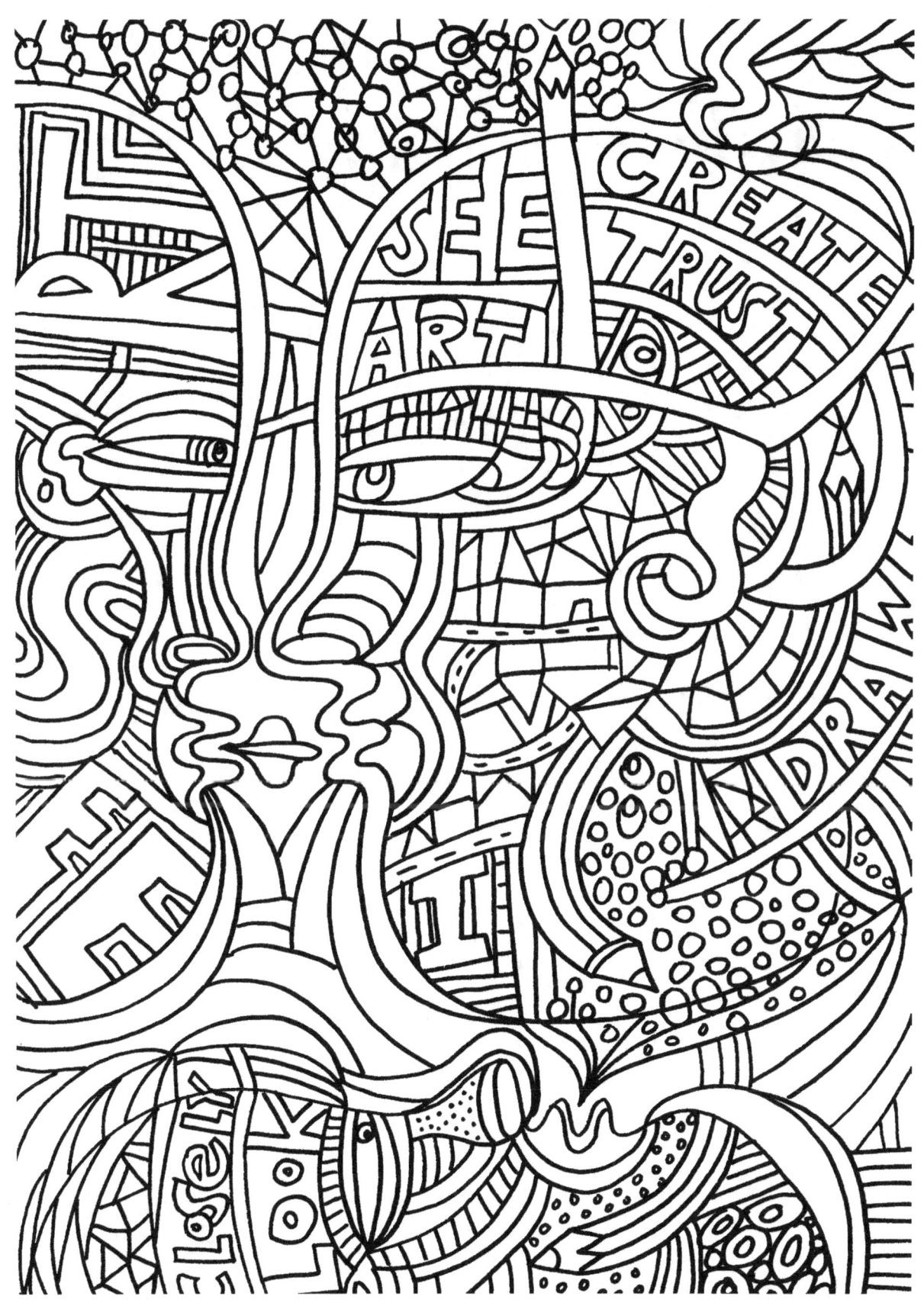

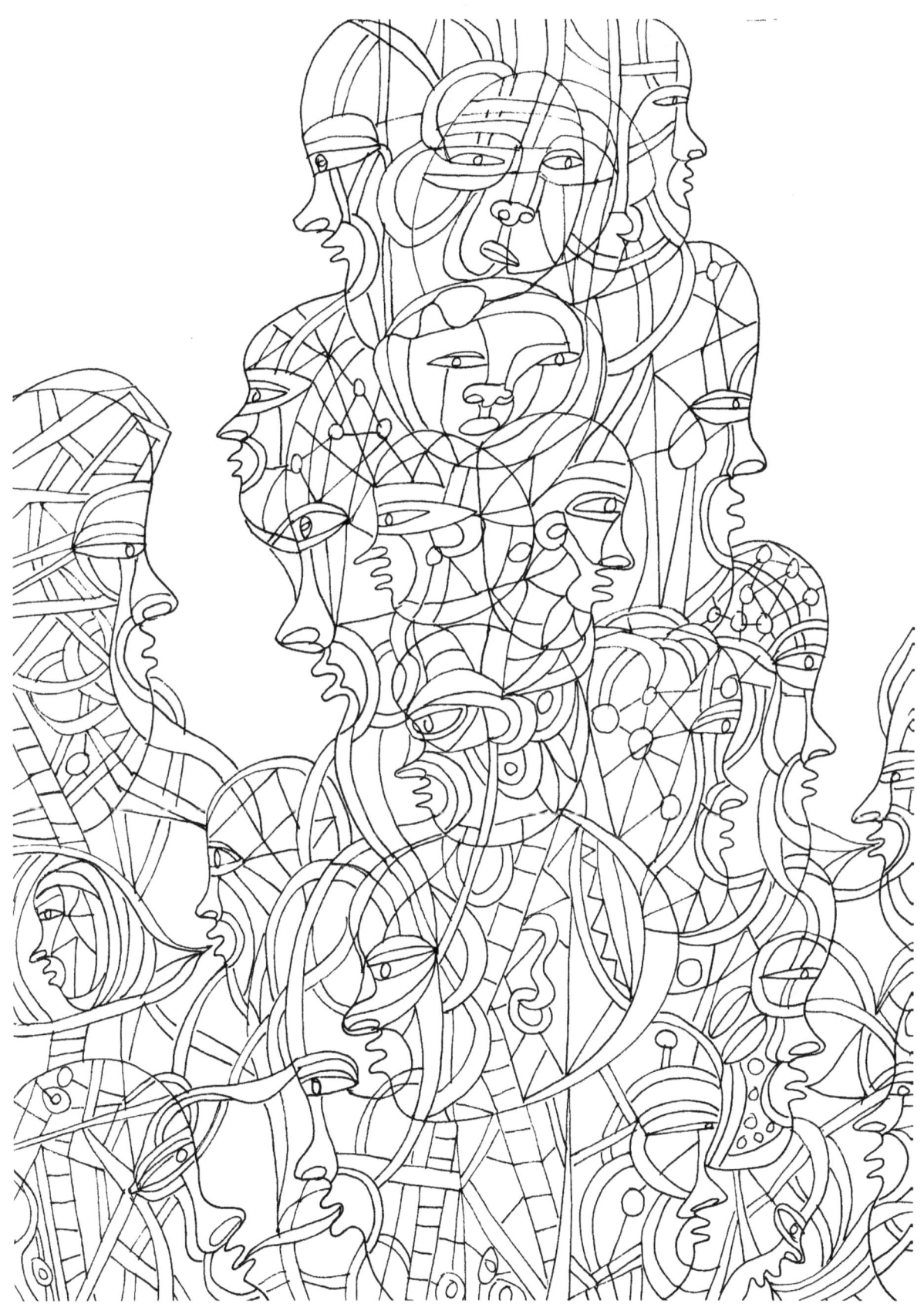

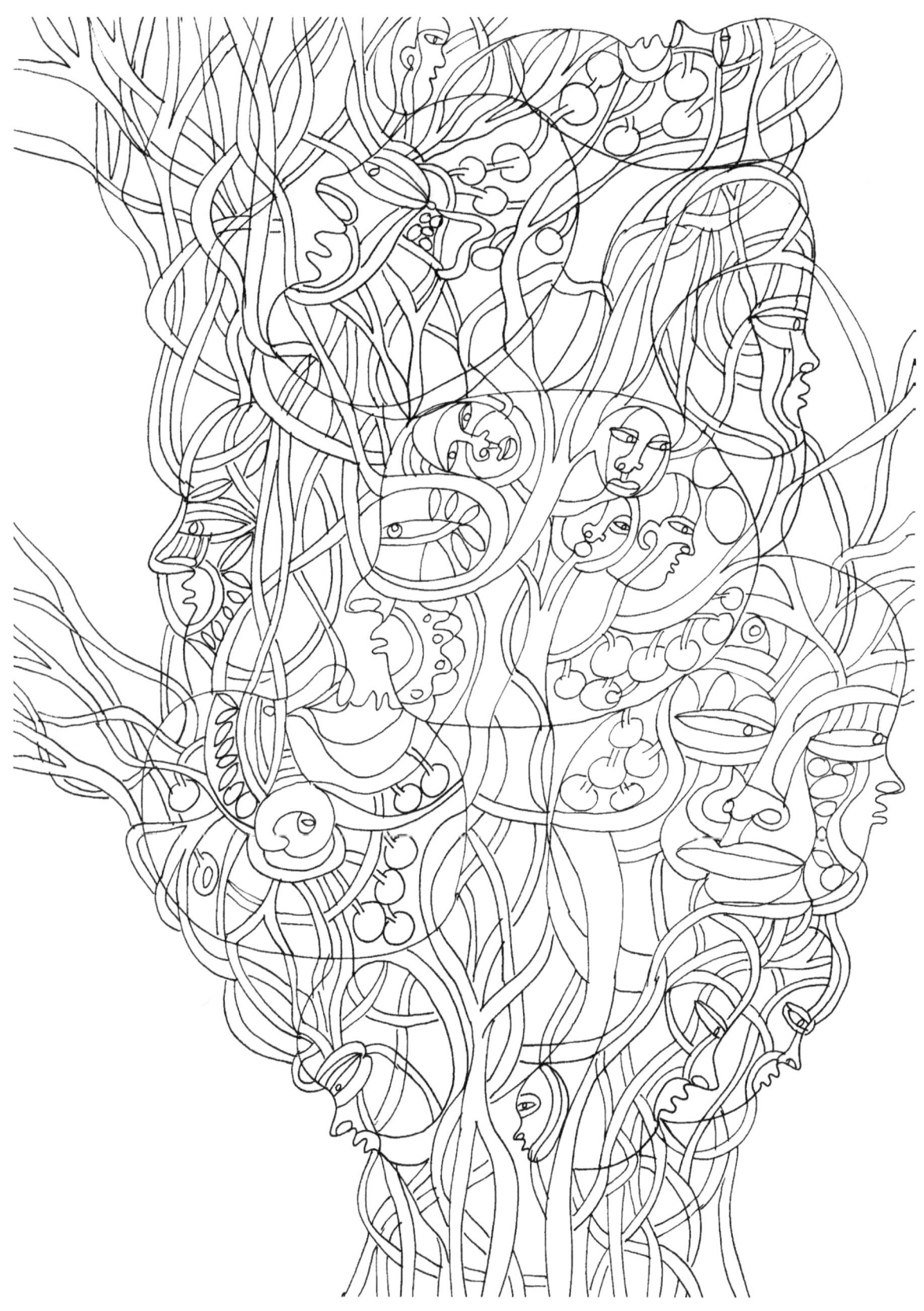

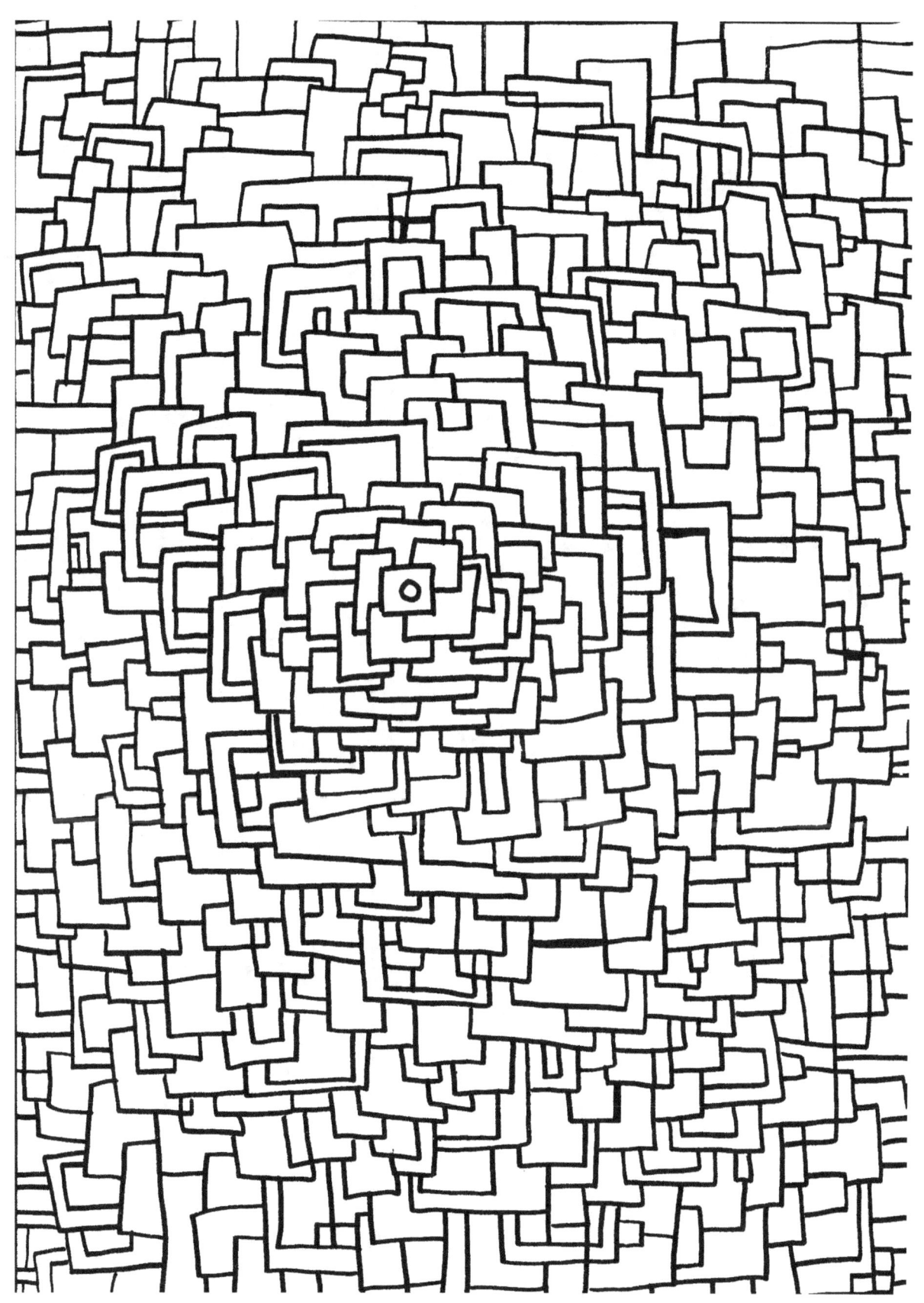

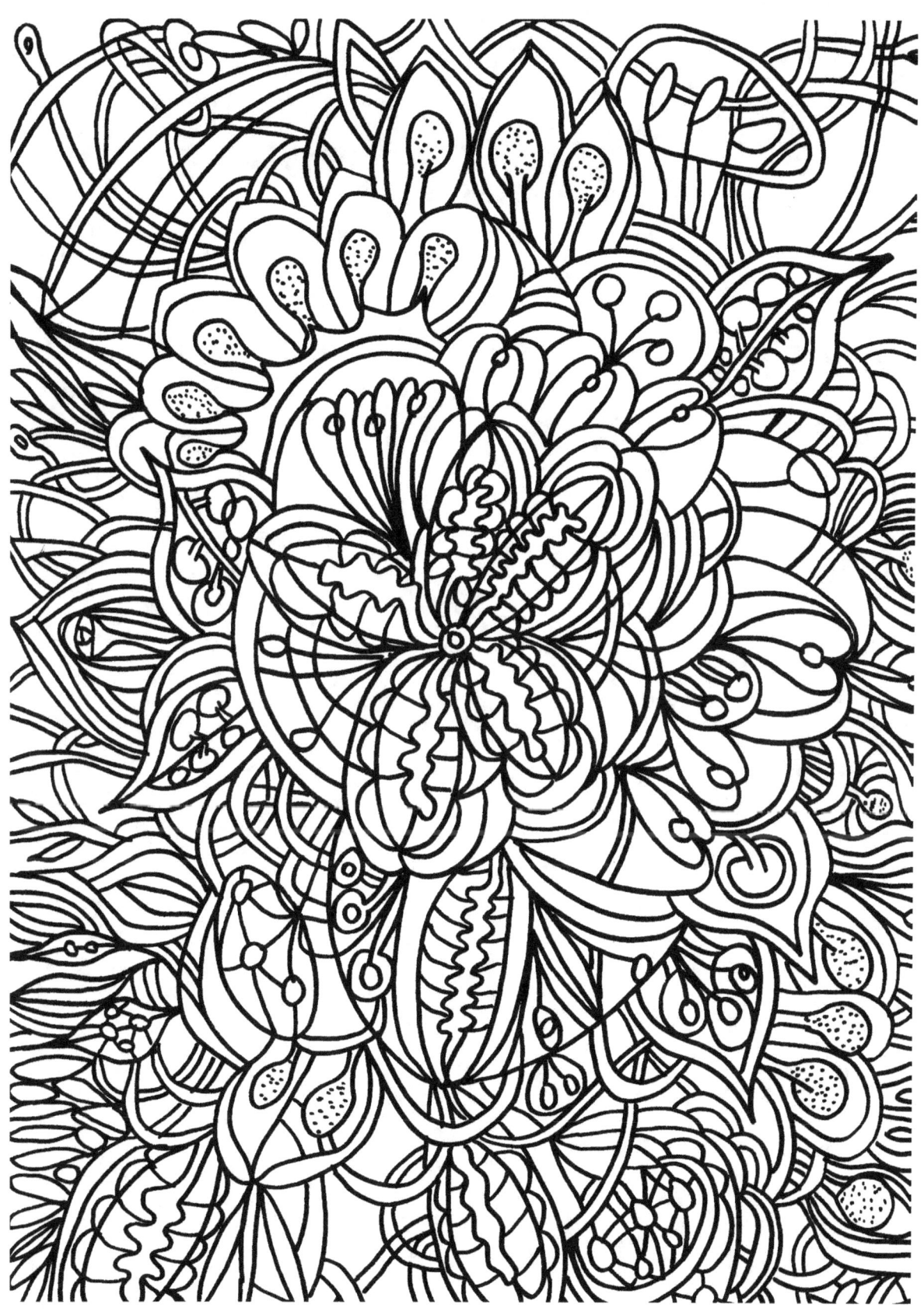

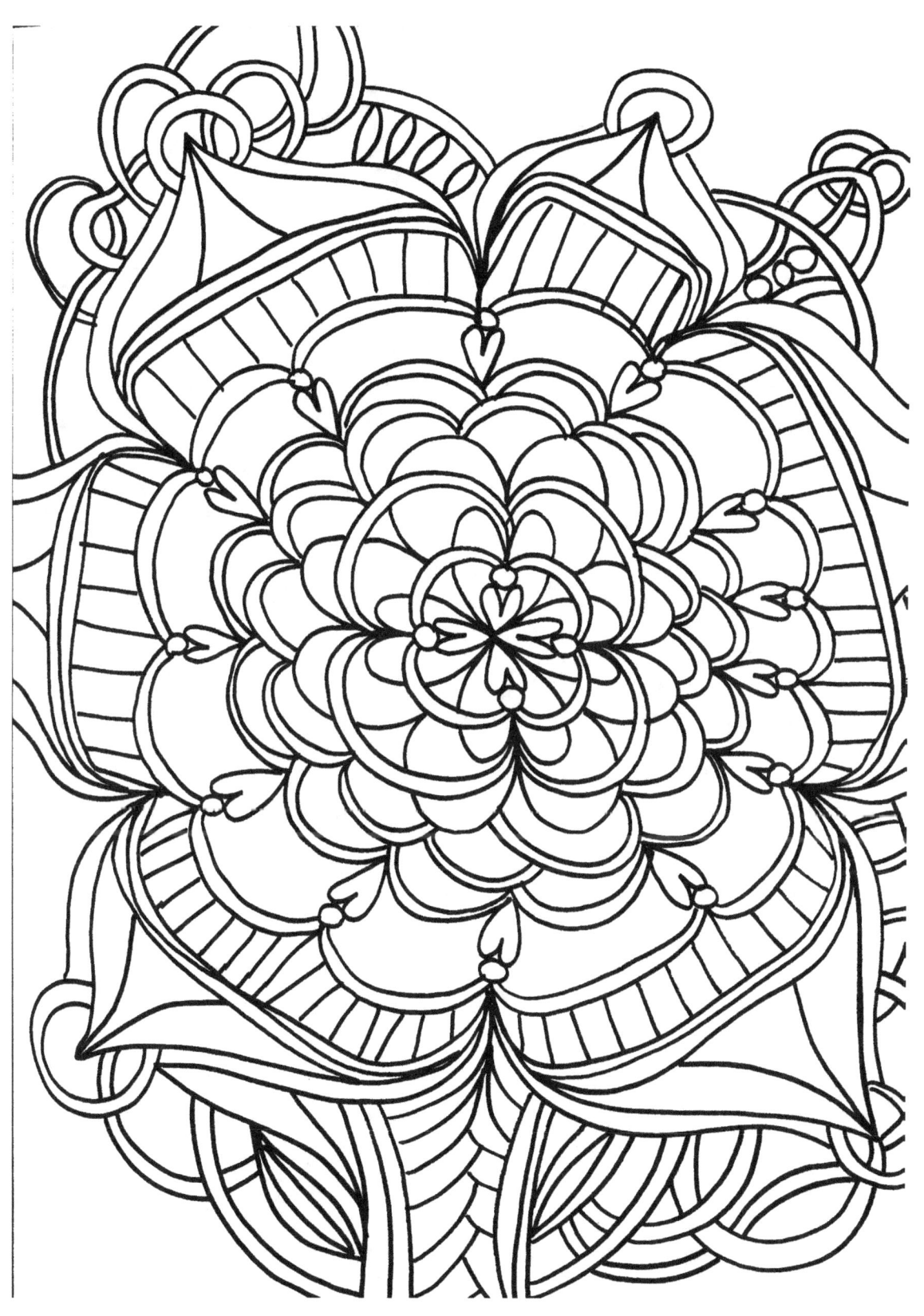

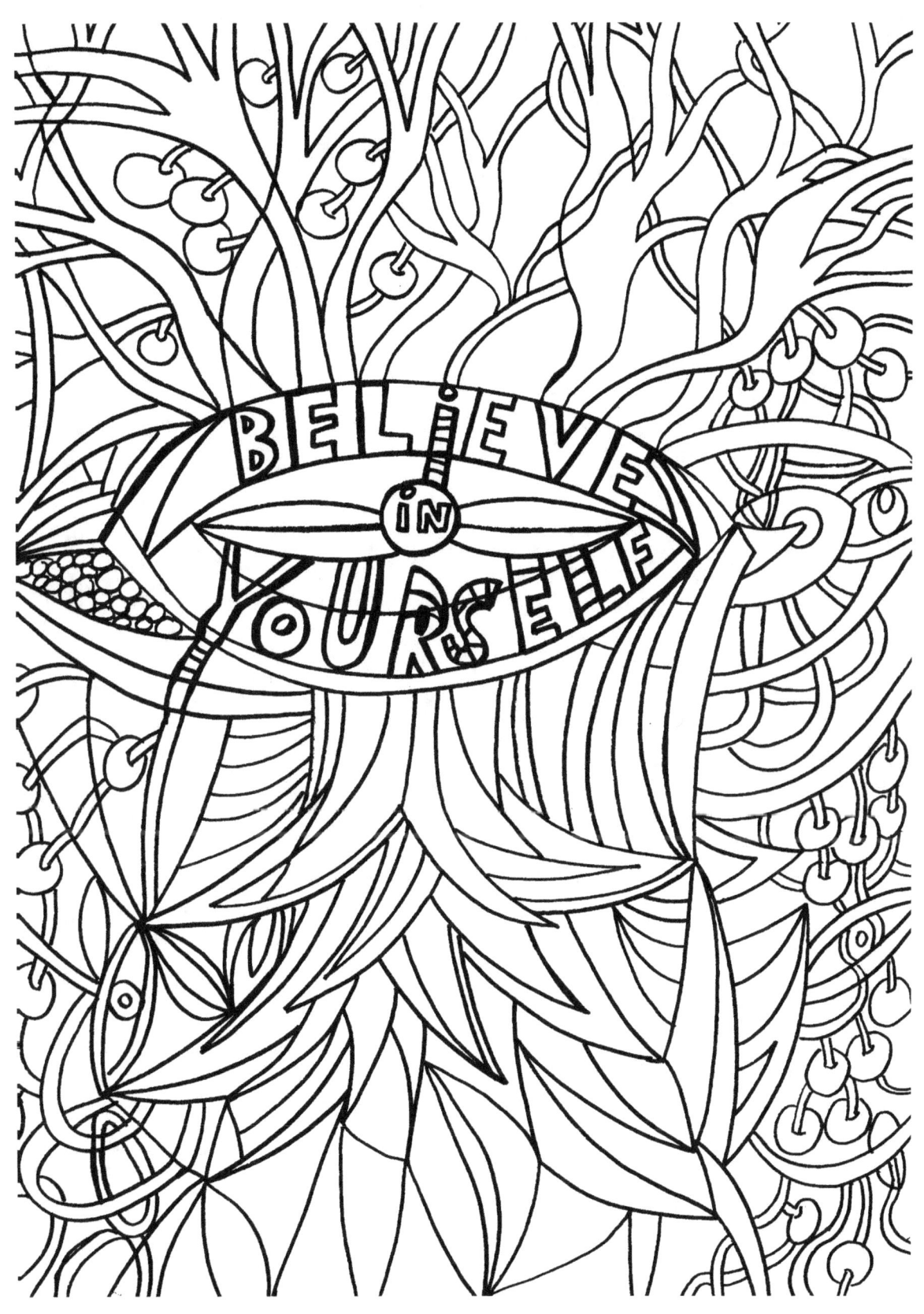

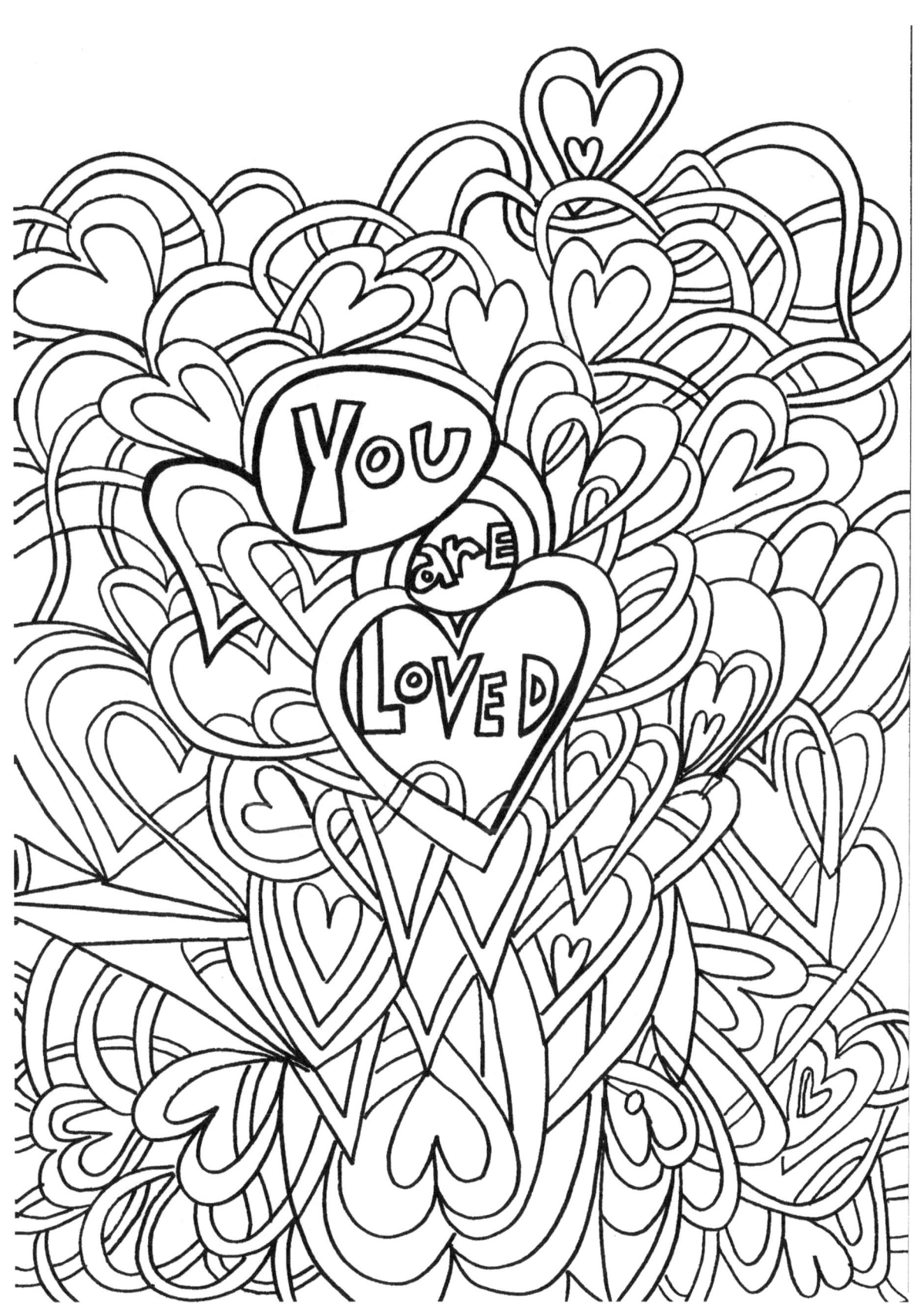

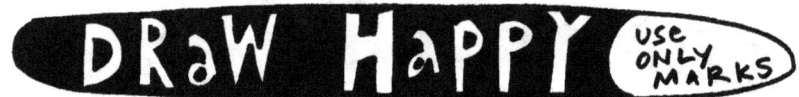

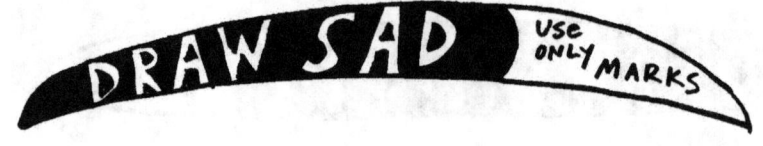

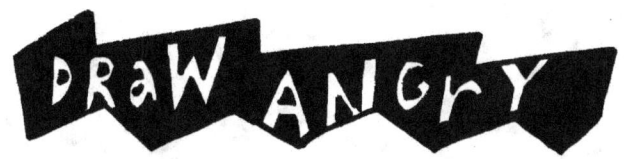

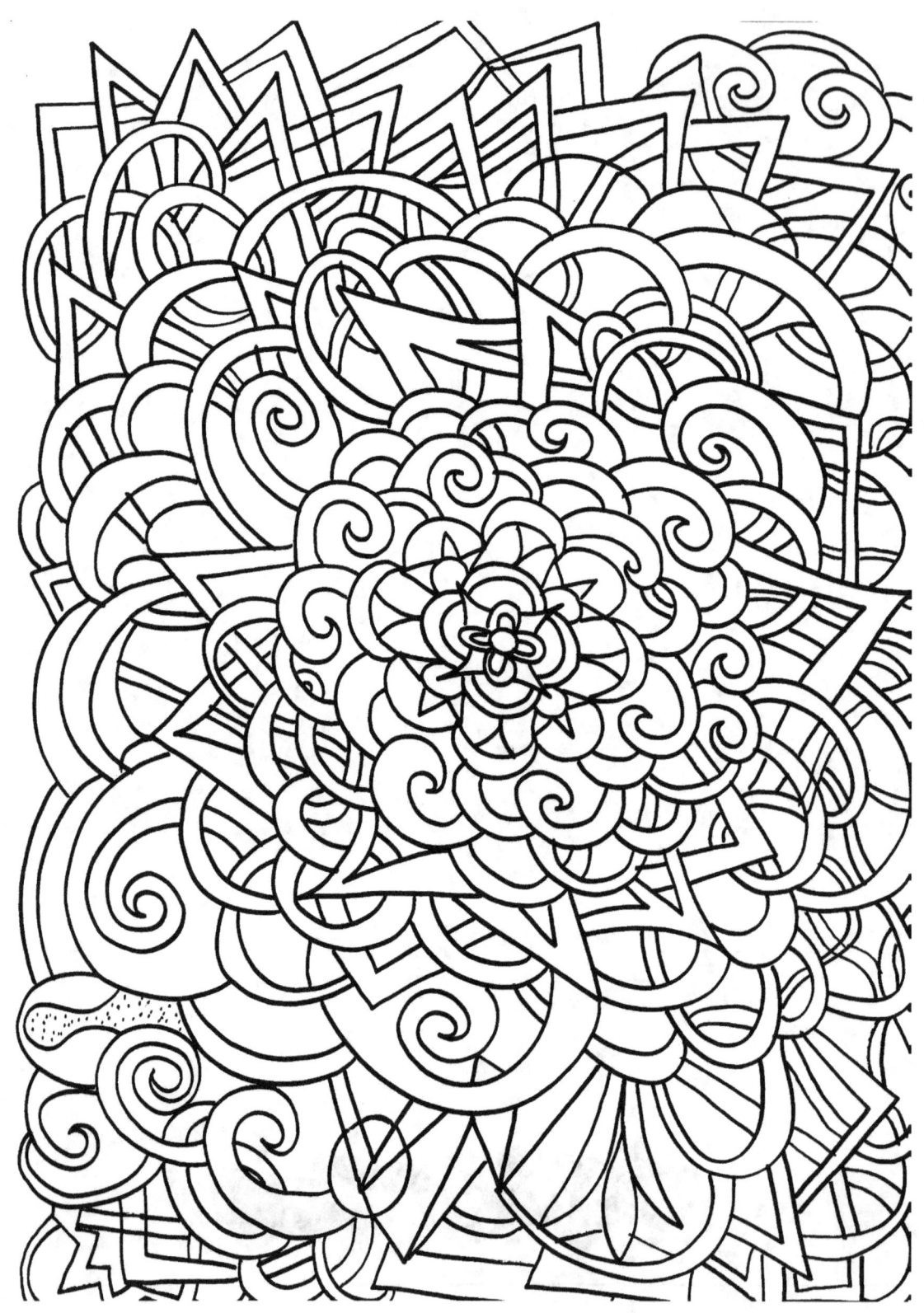

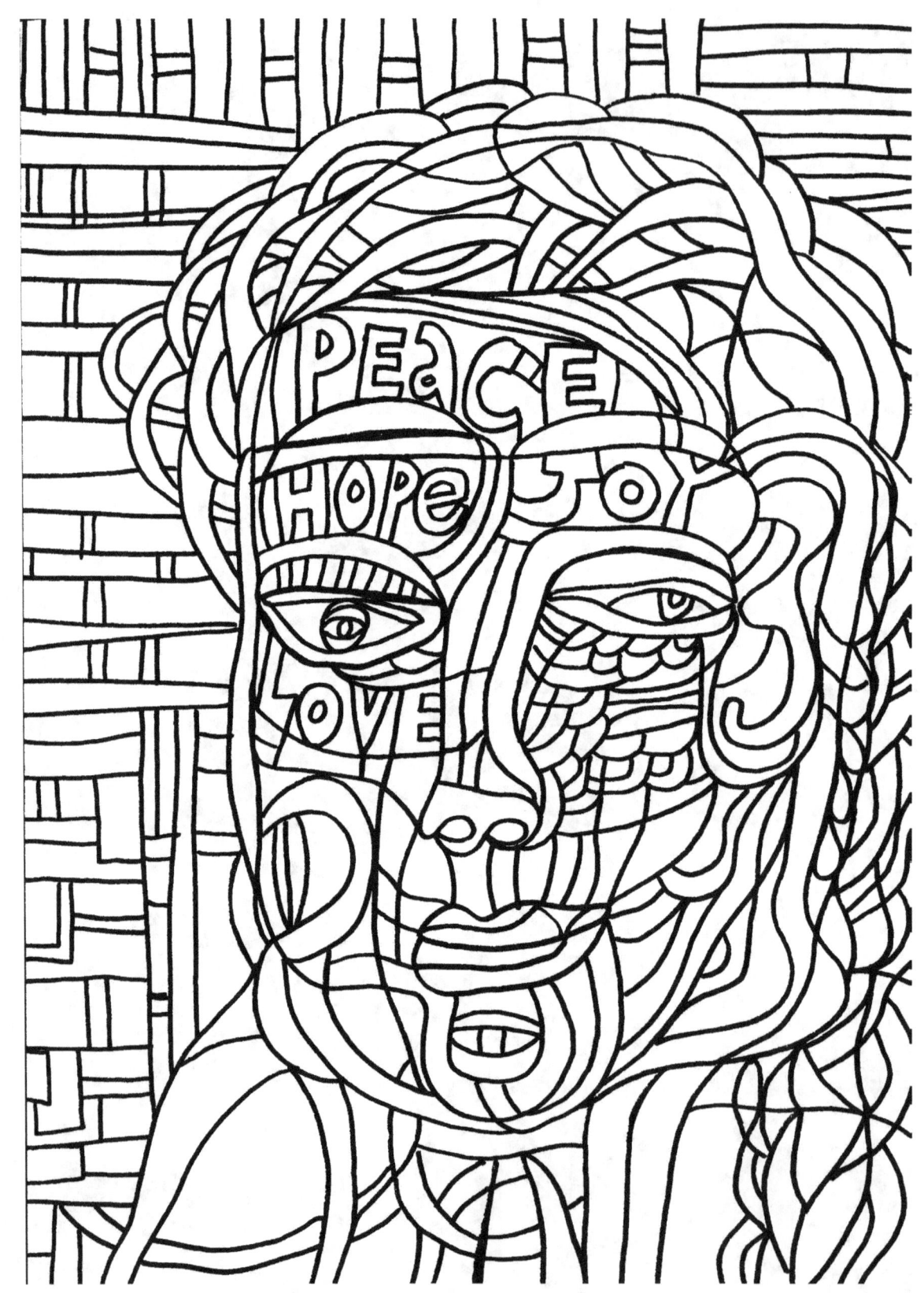

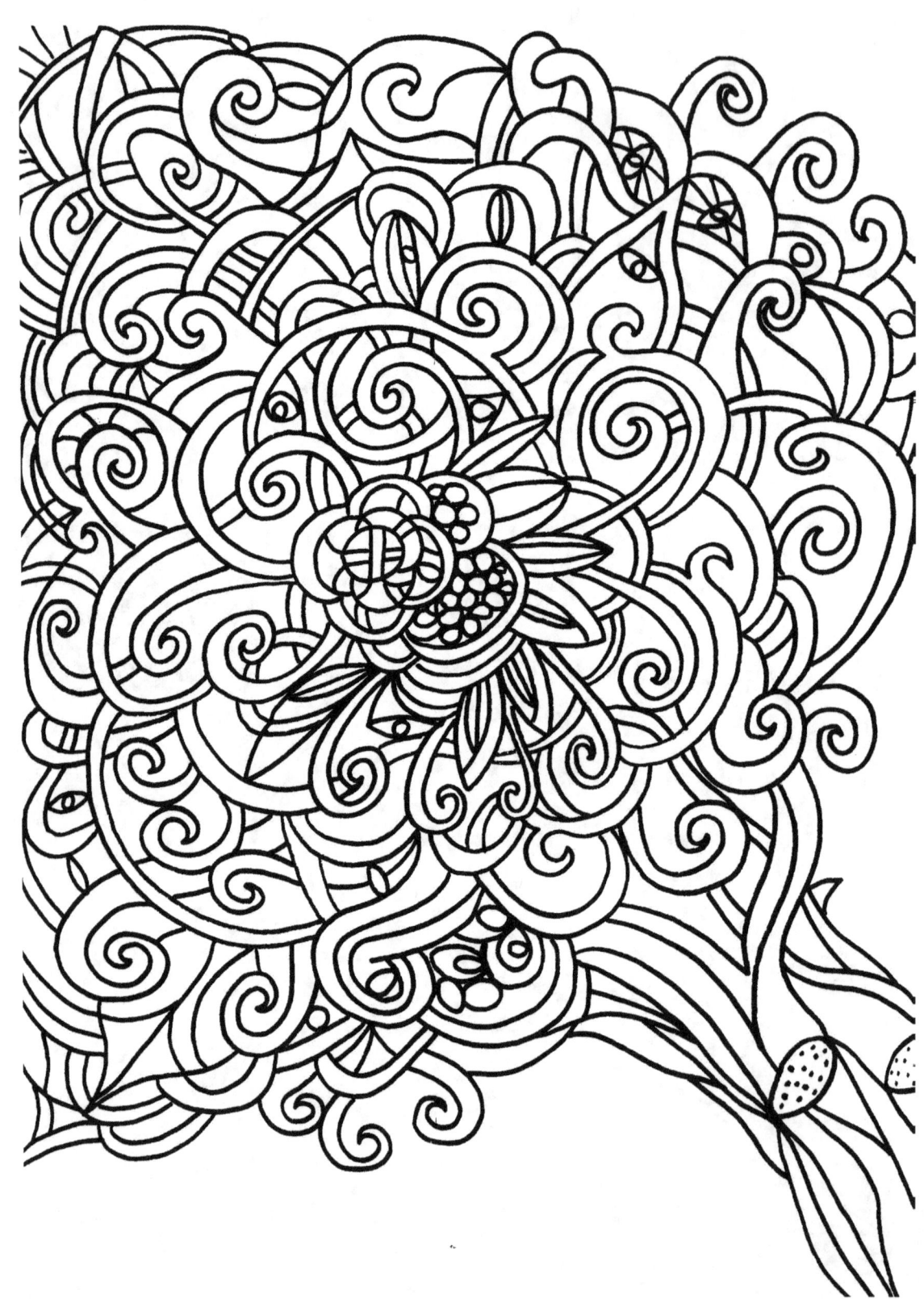

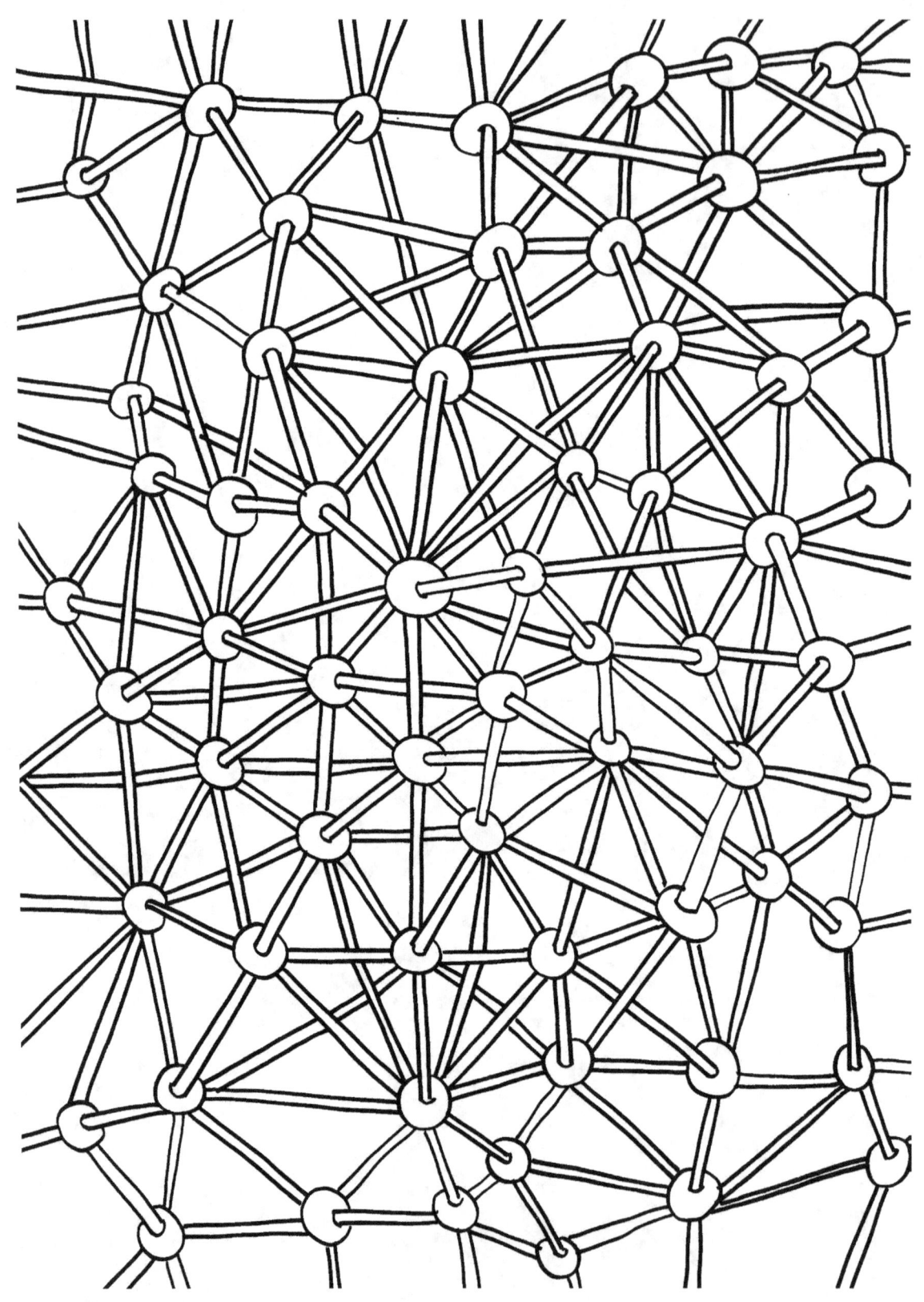

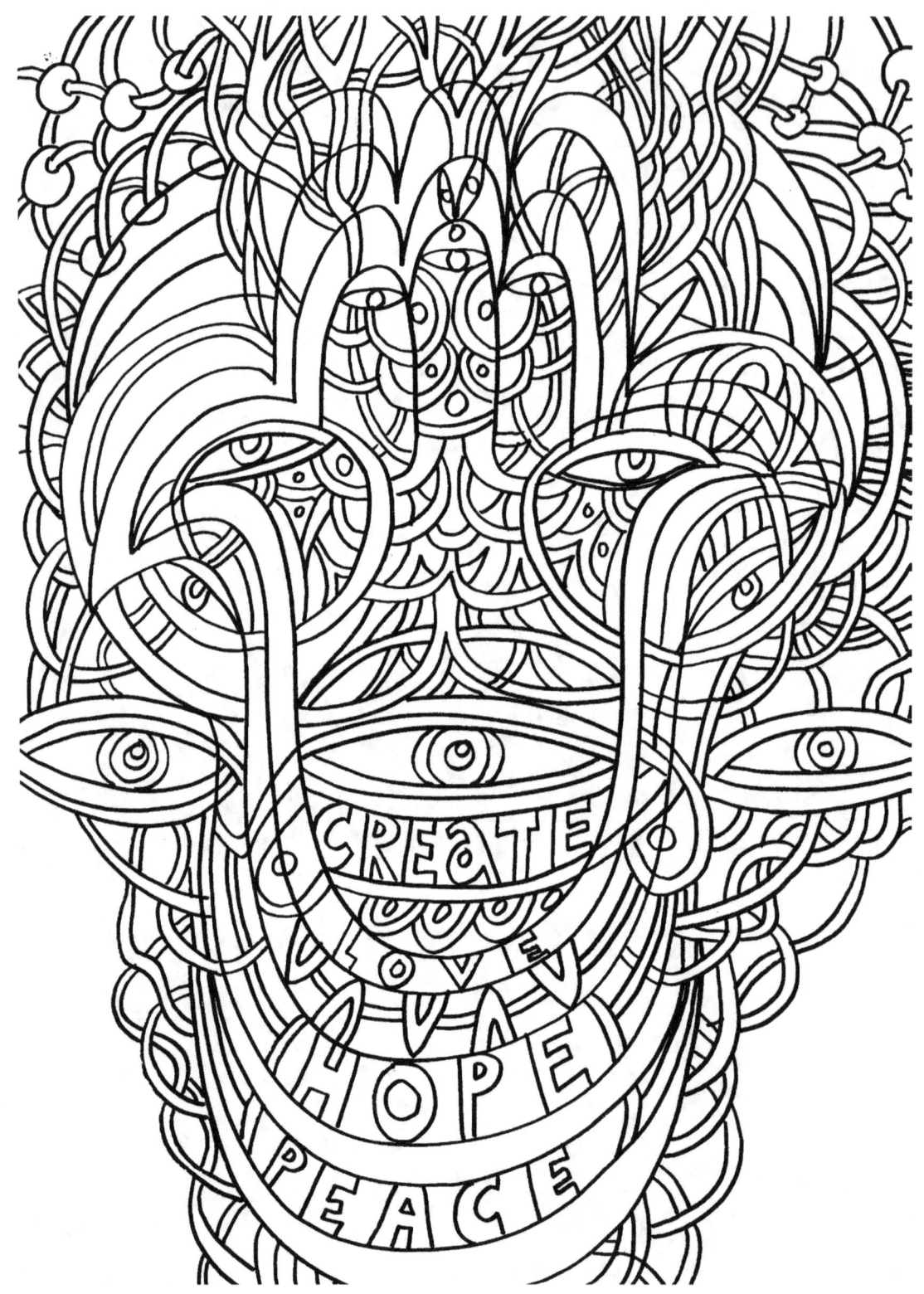

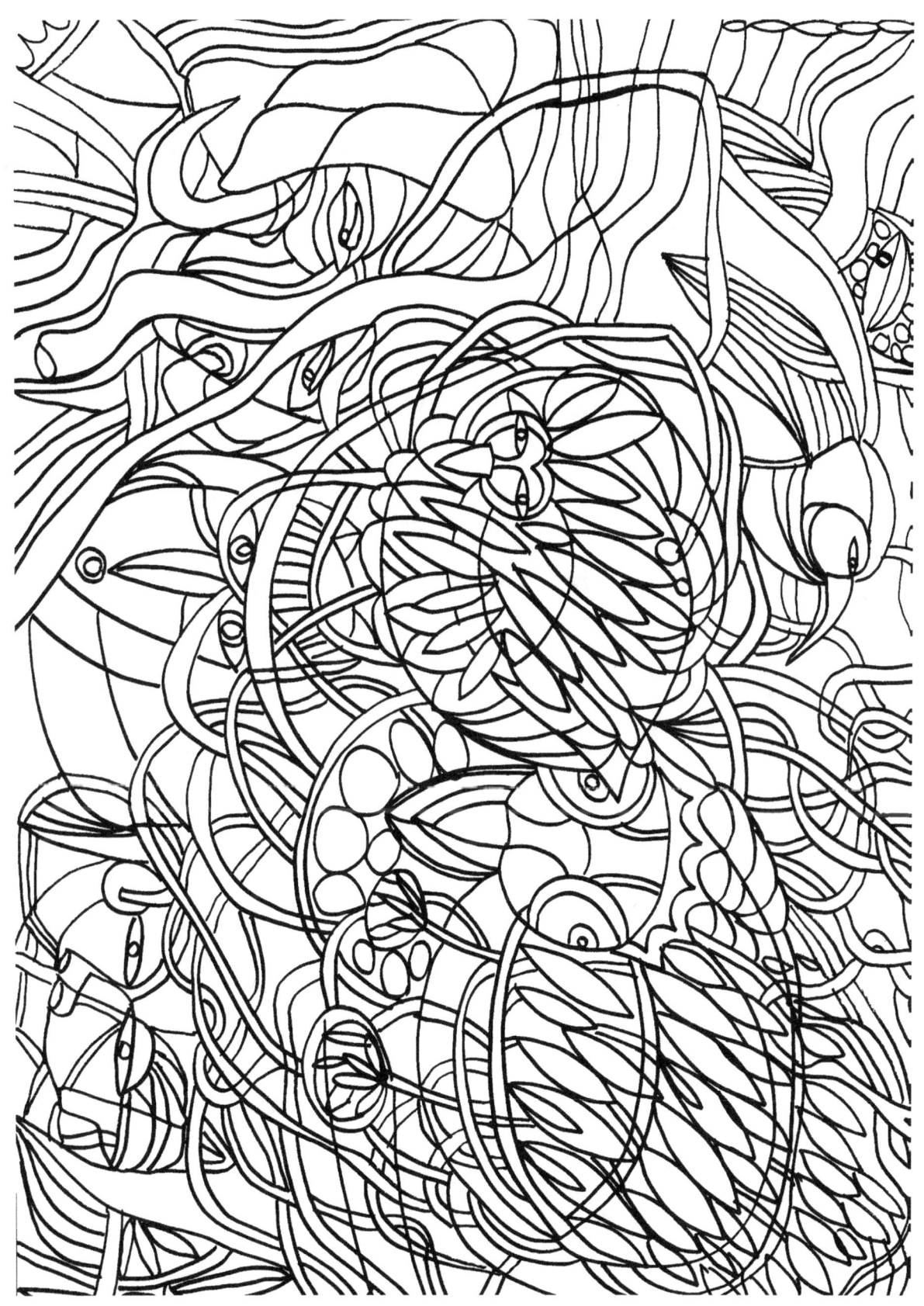

DRAW TO JAZZ MUSIC

DRaw to CLaSSiCaL MUSiC

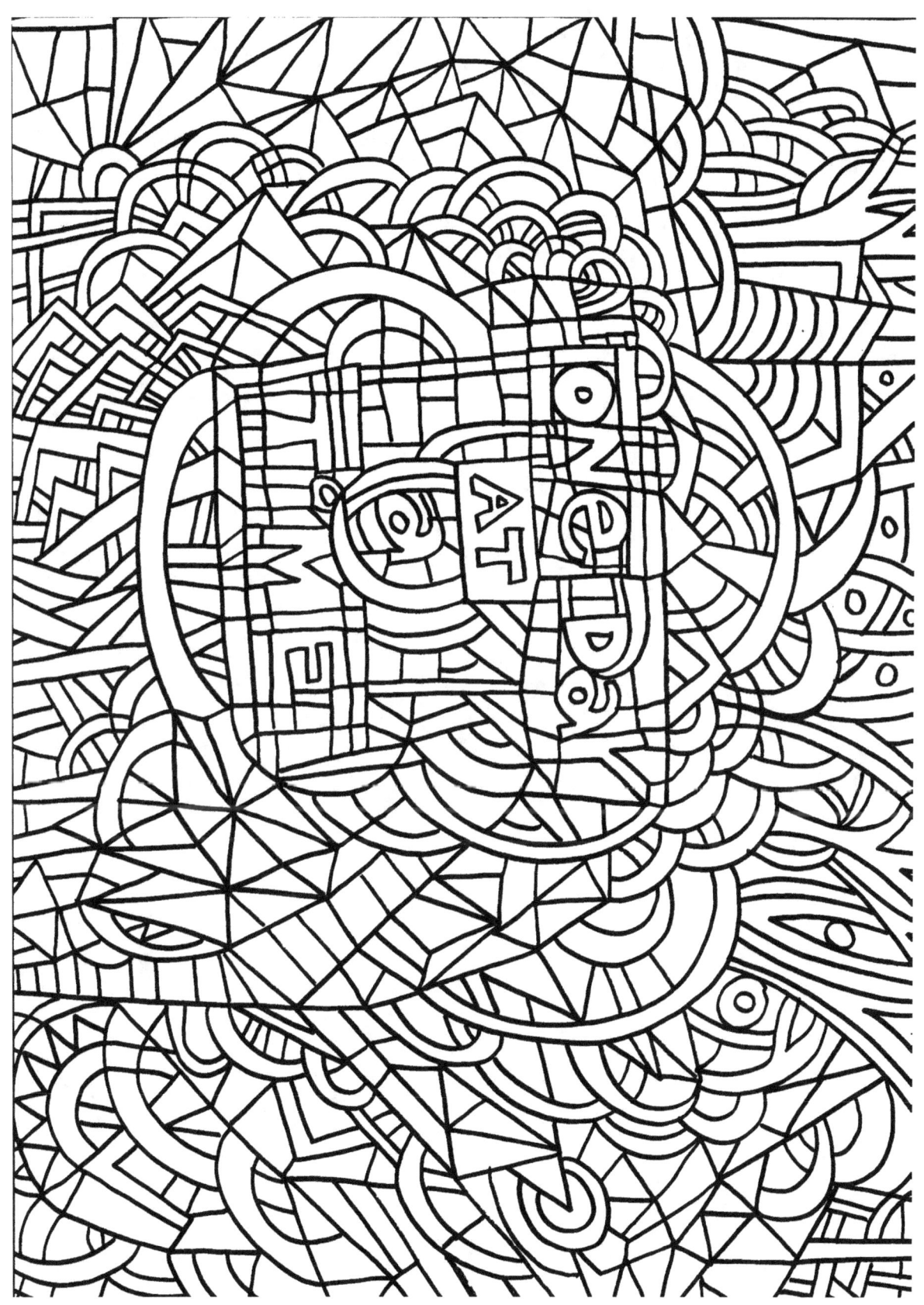

DRAW the SOUNDS OUTSIDE

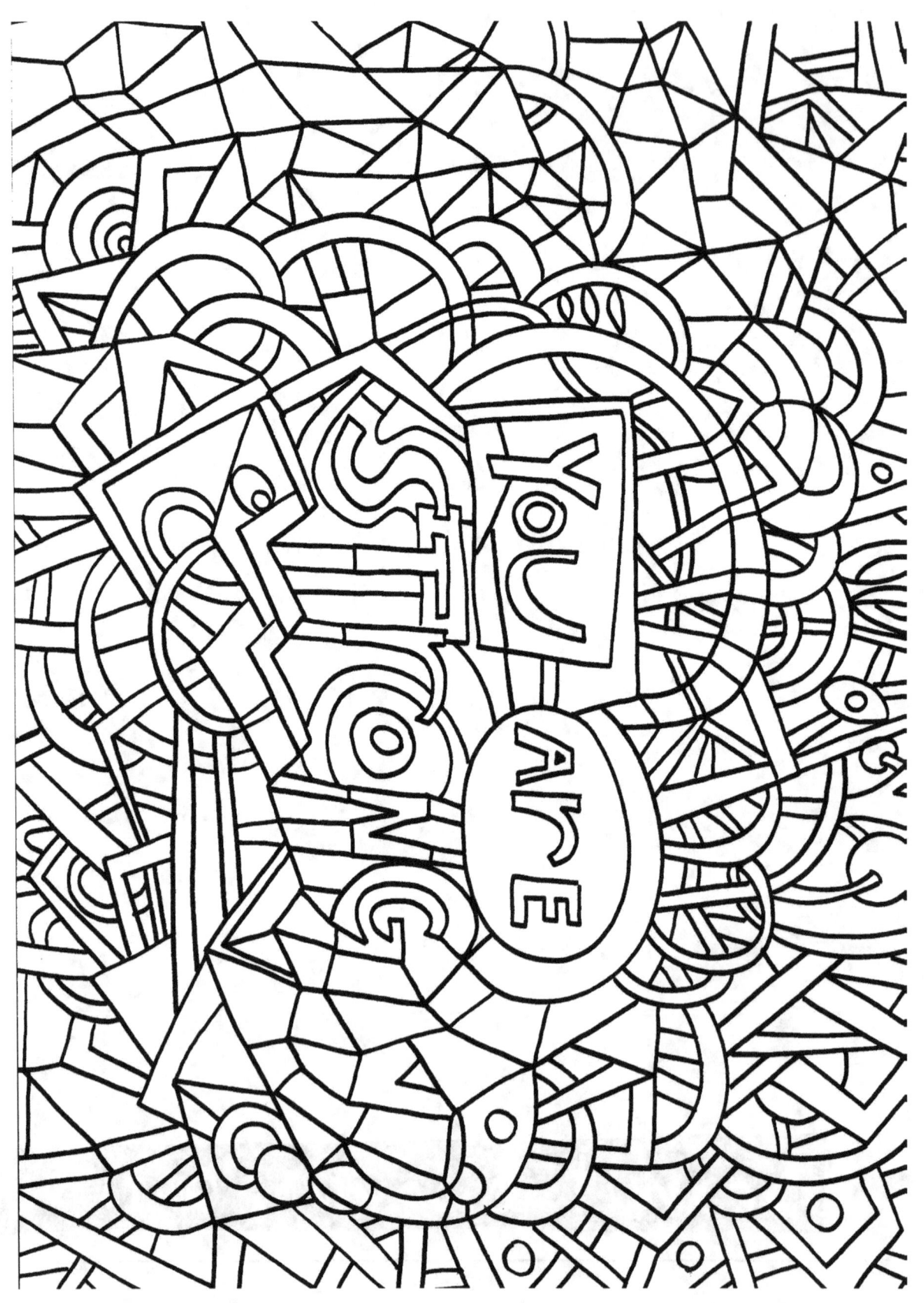

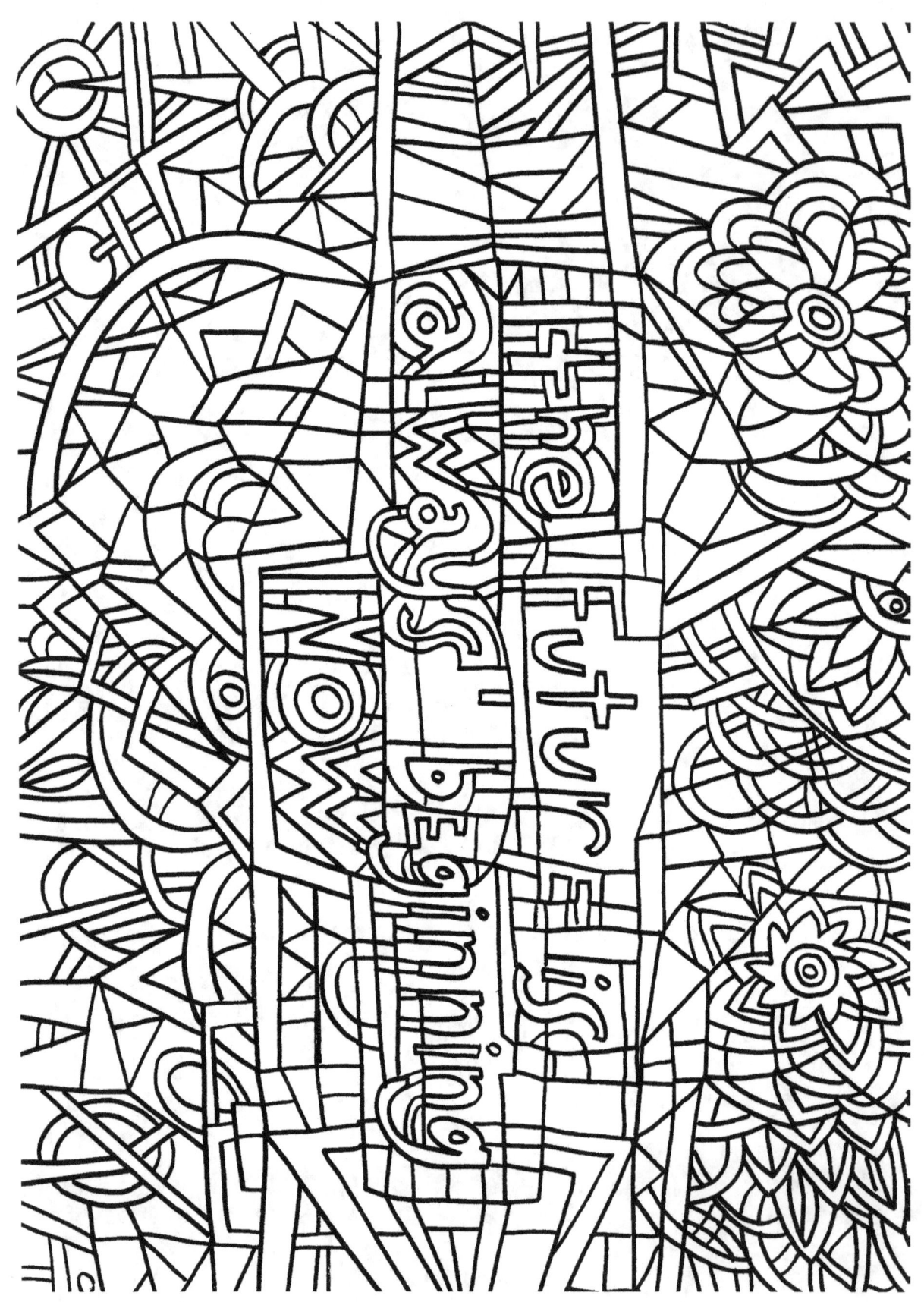

the future is always beginning now

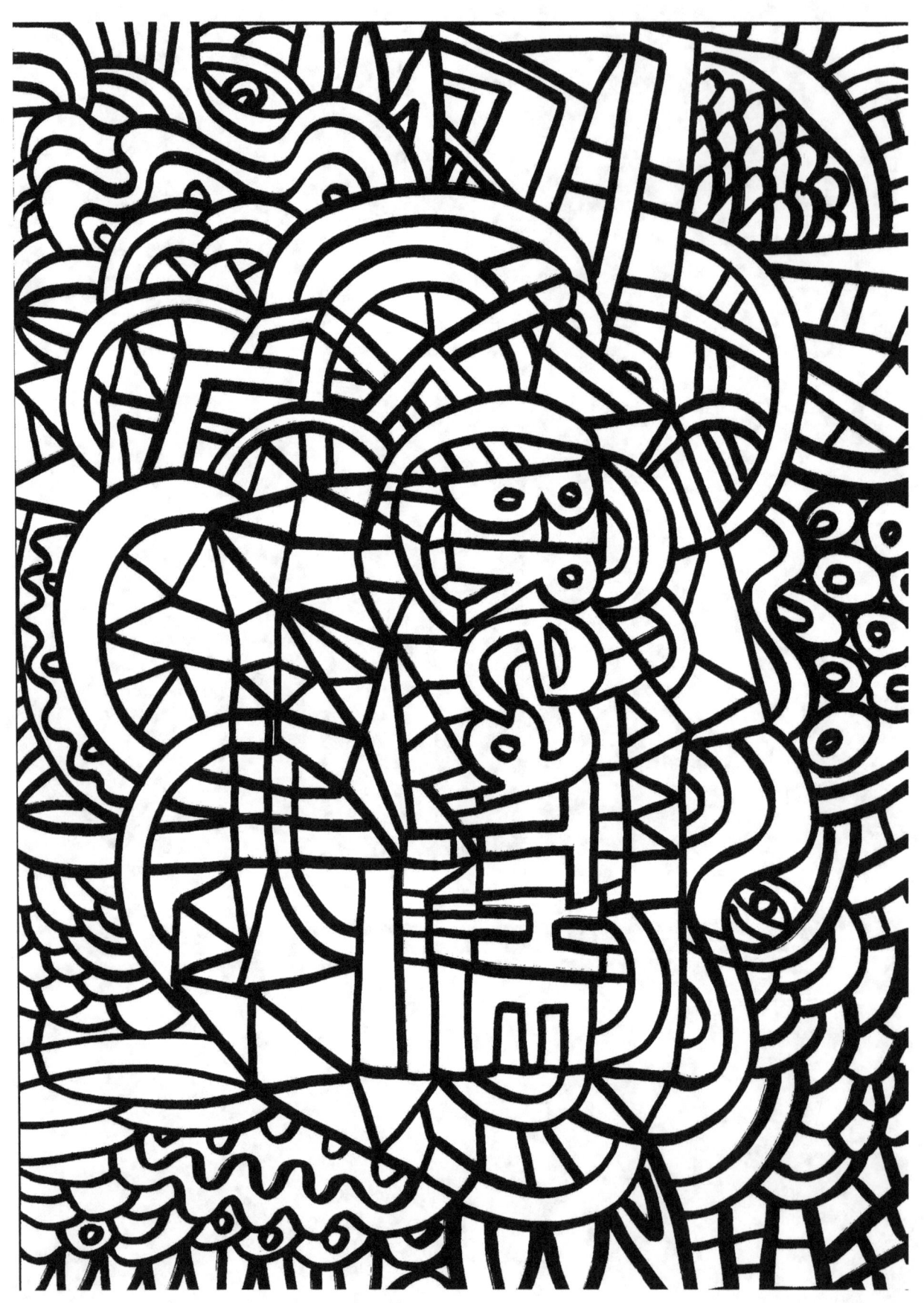

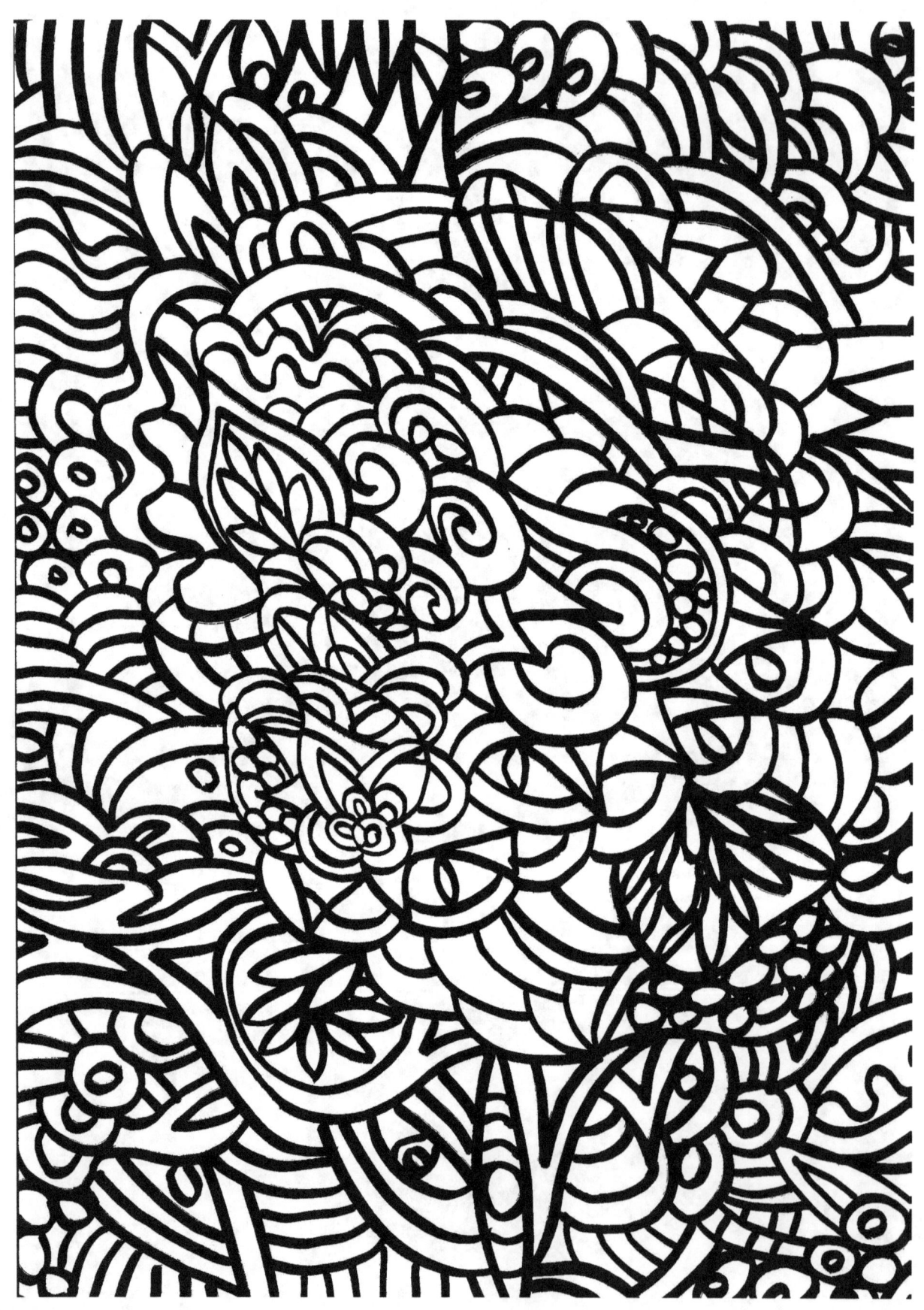

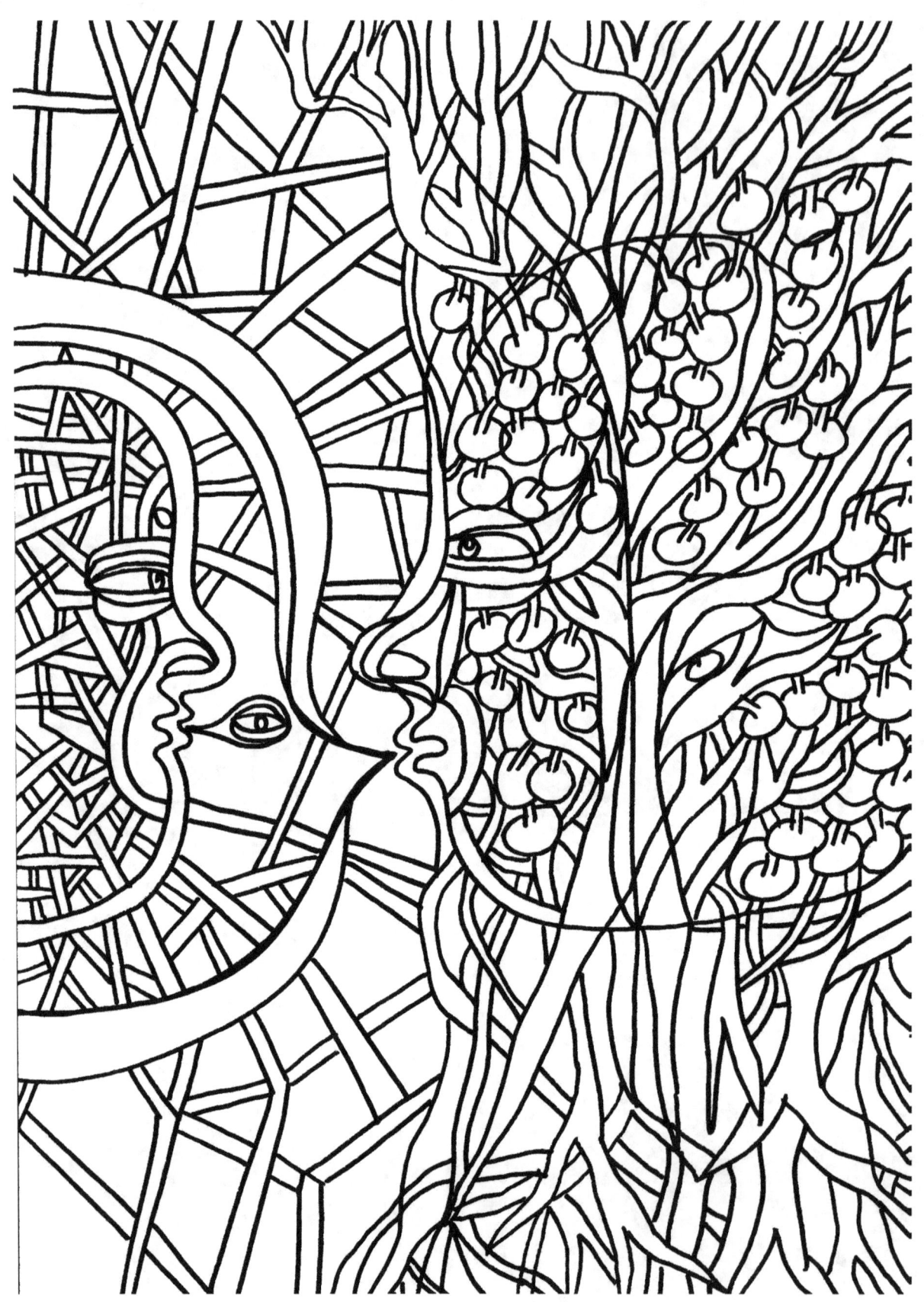

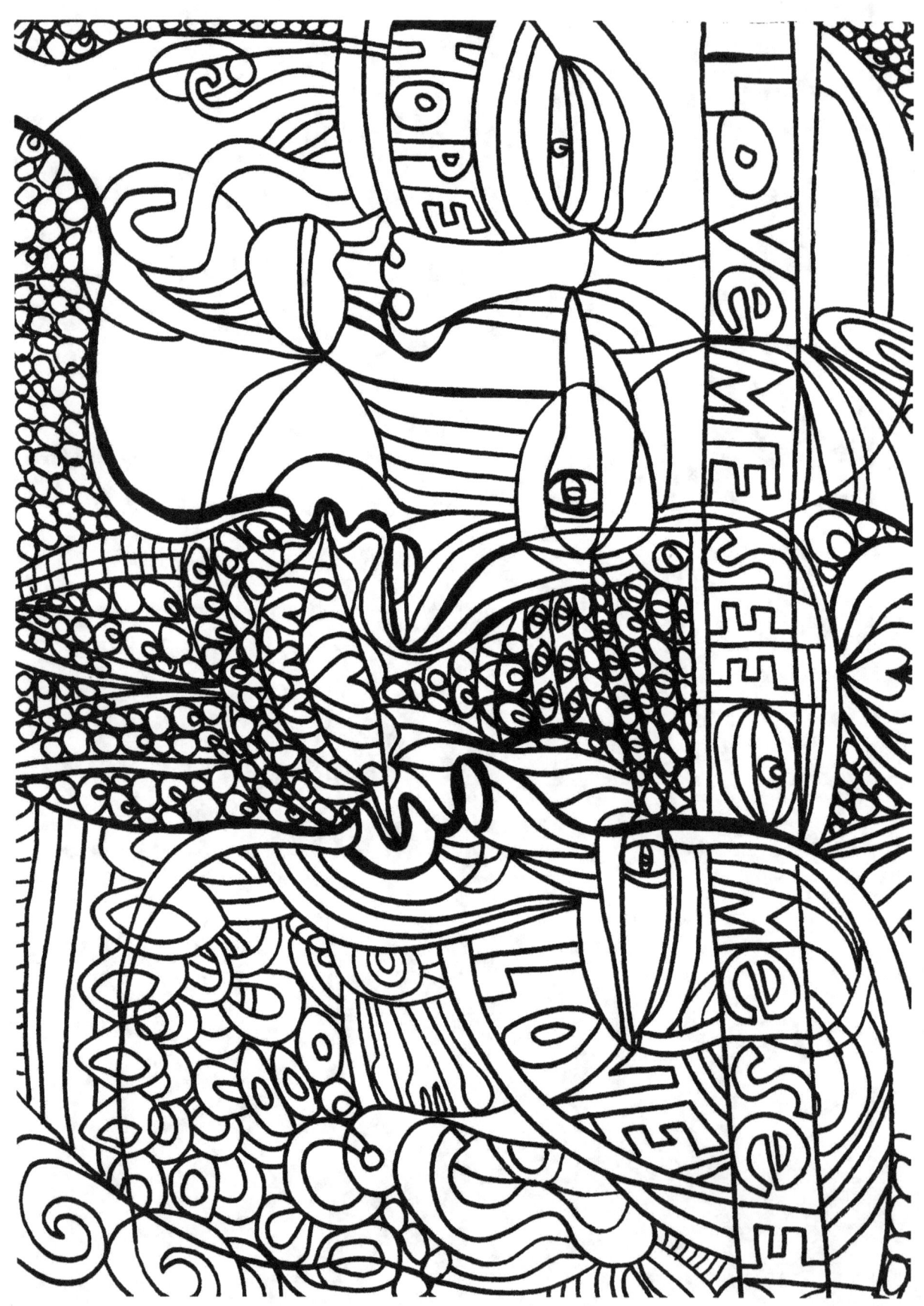

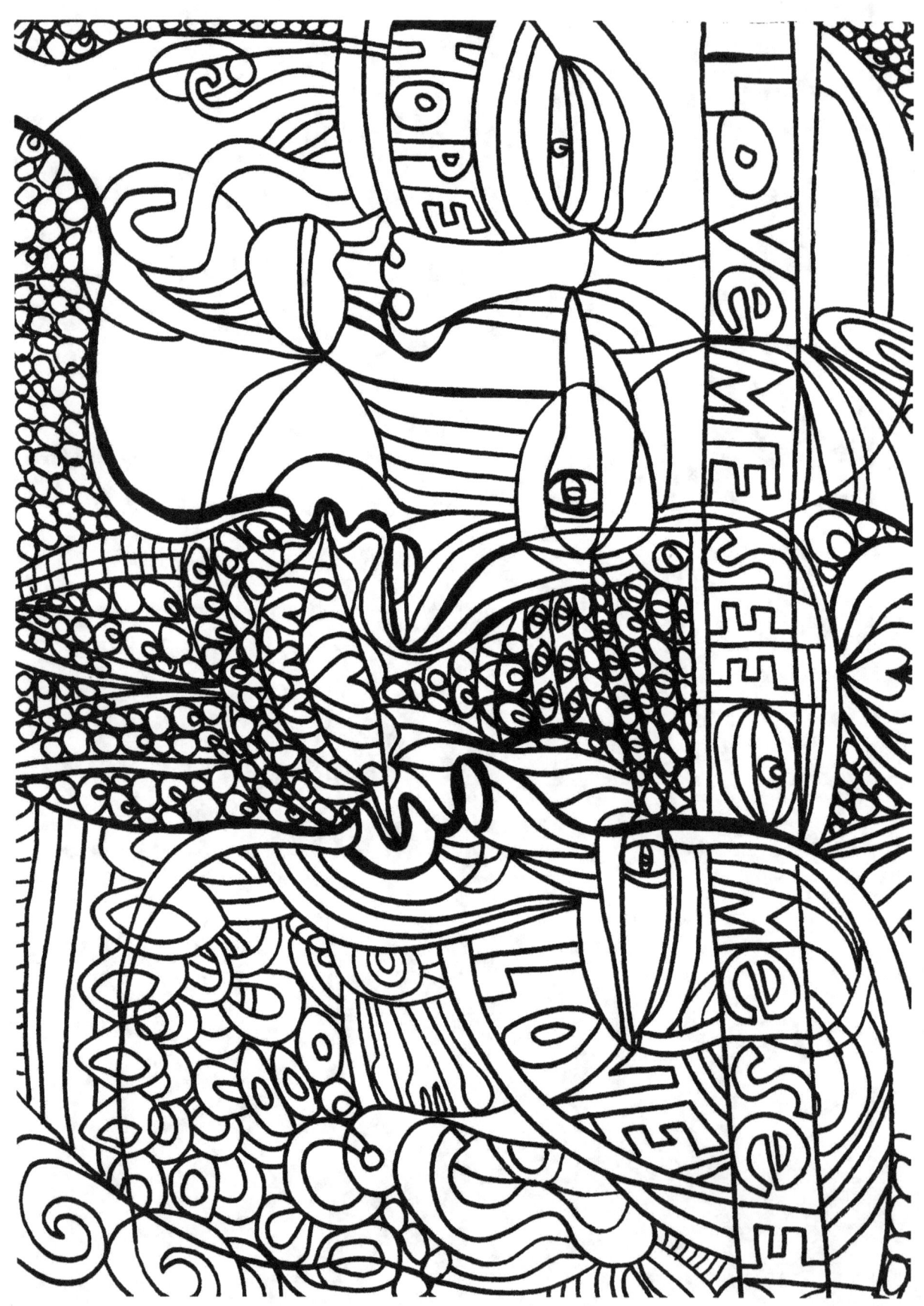
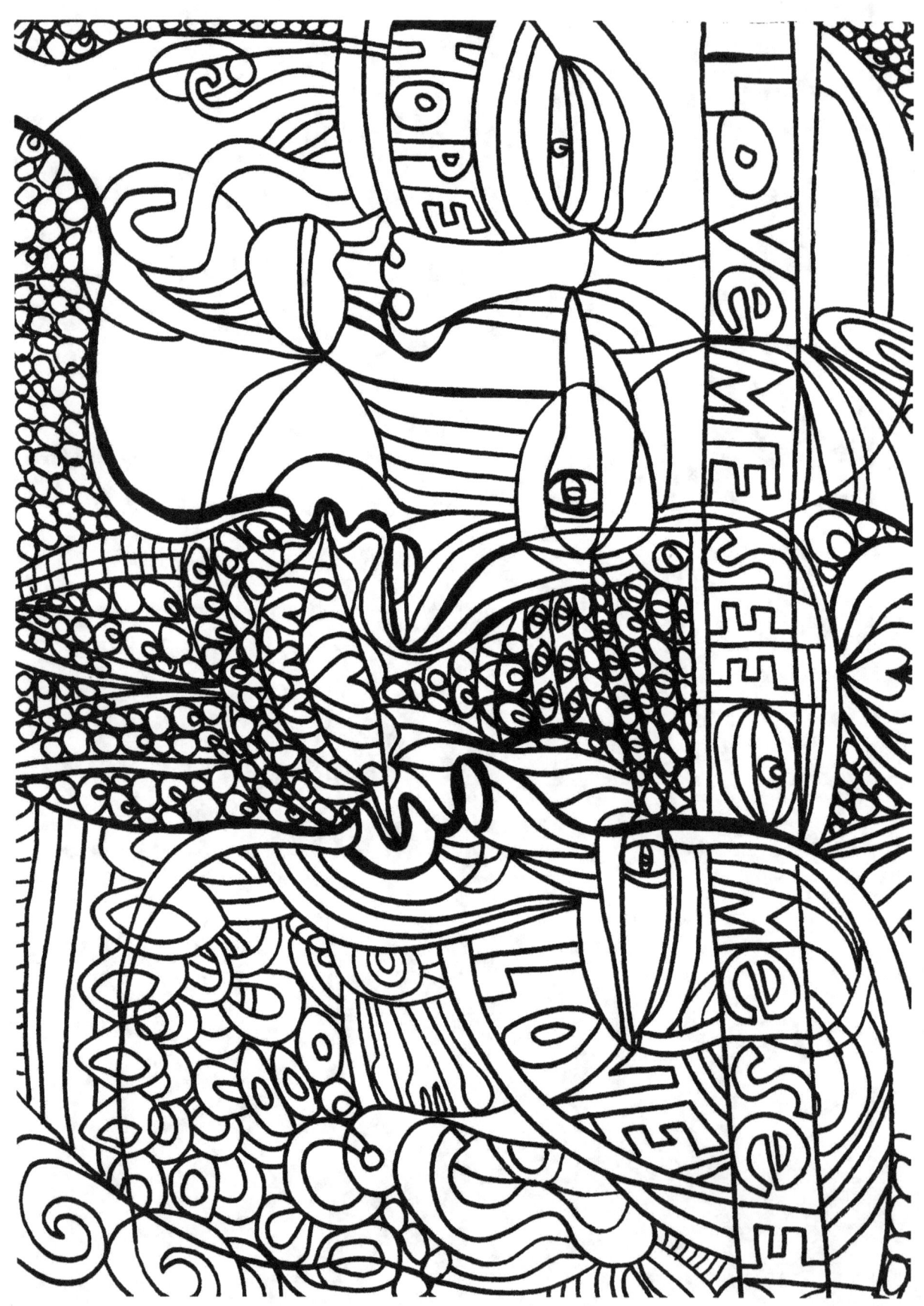

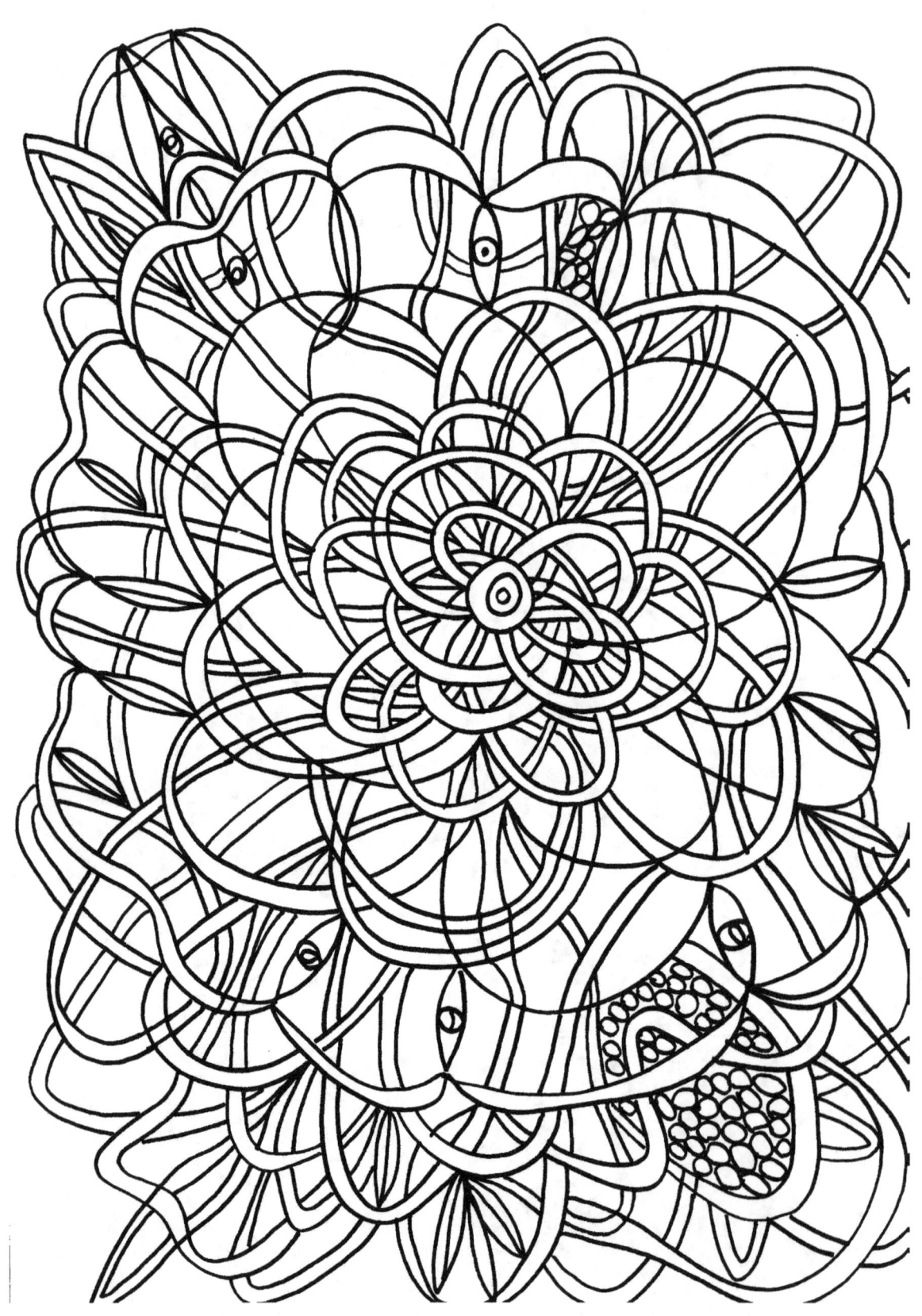

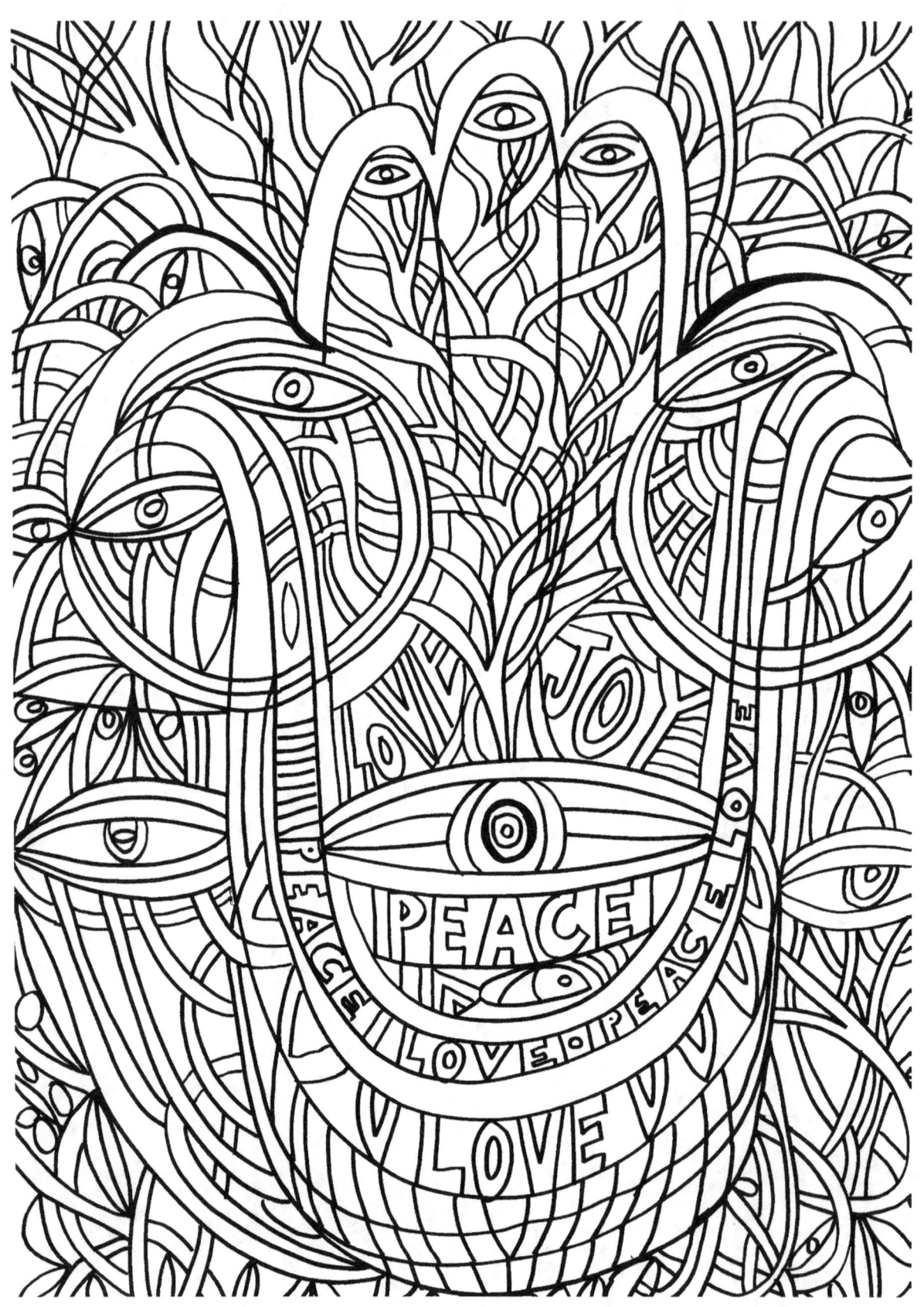

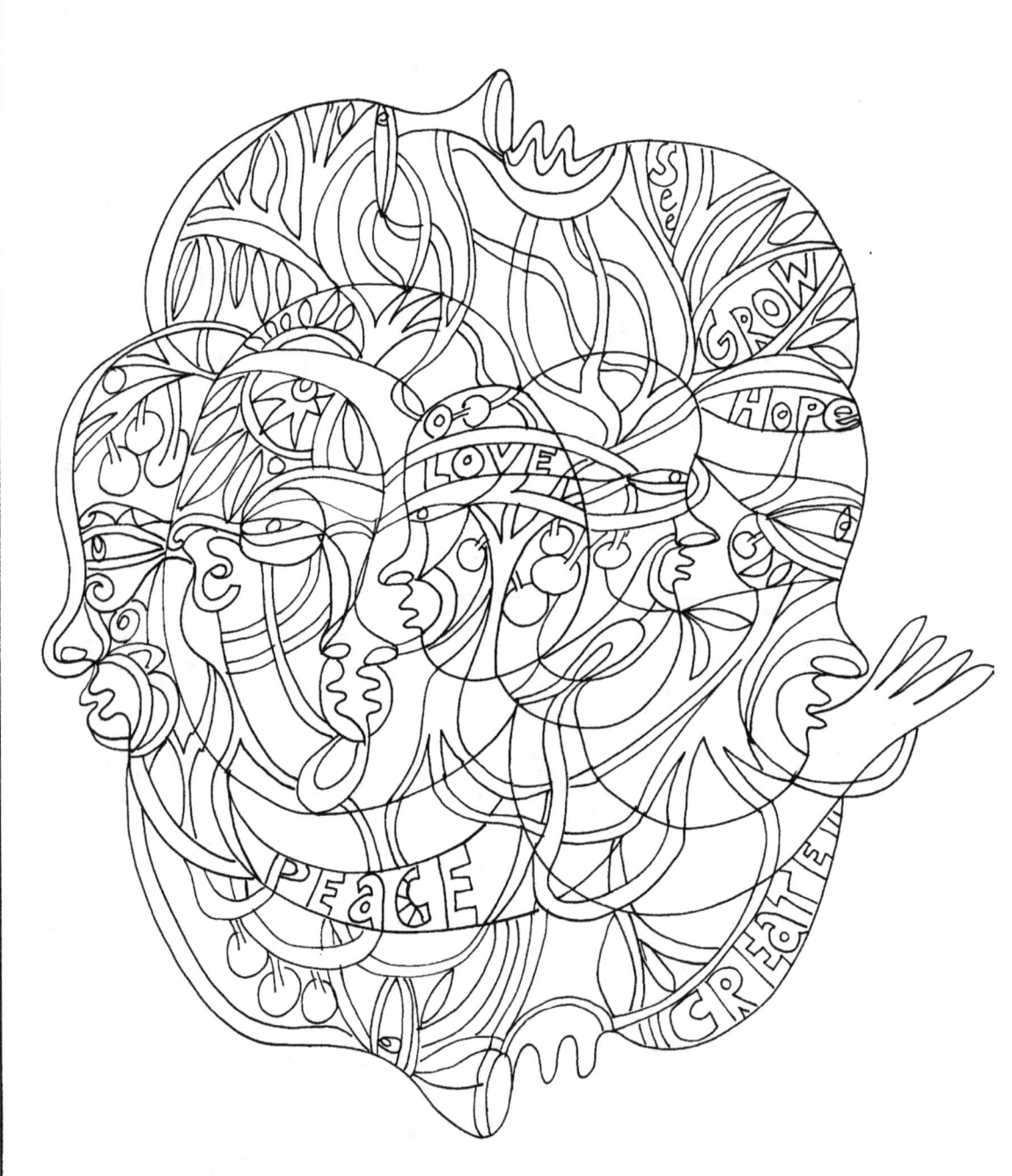

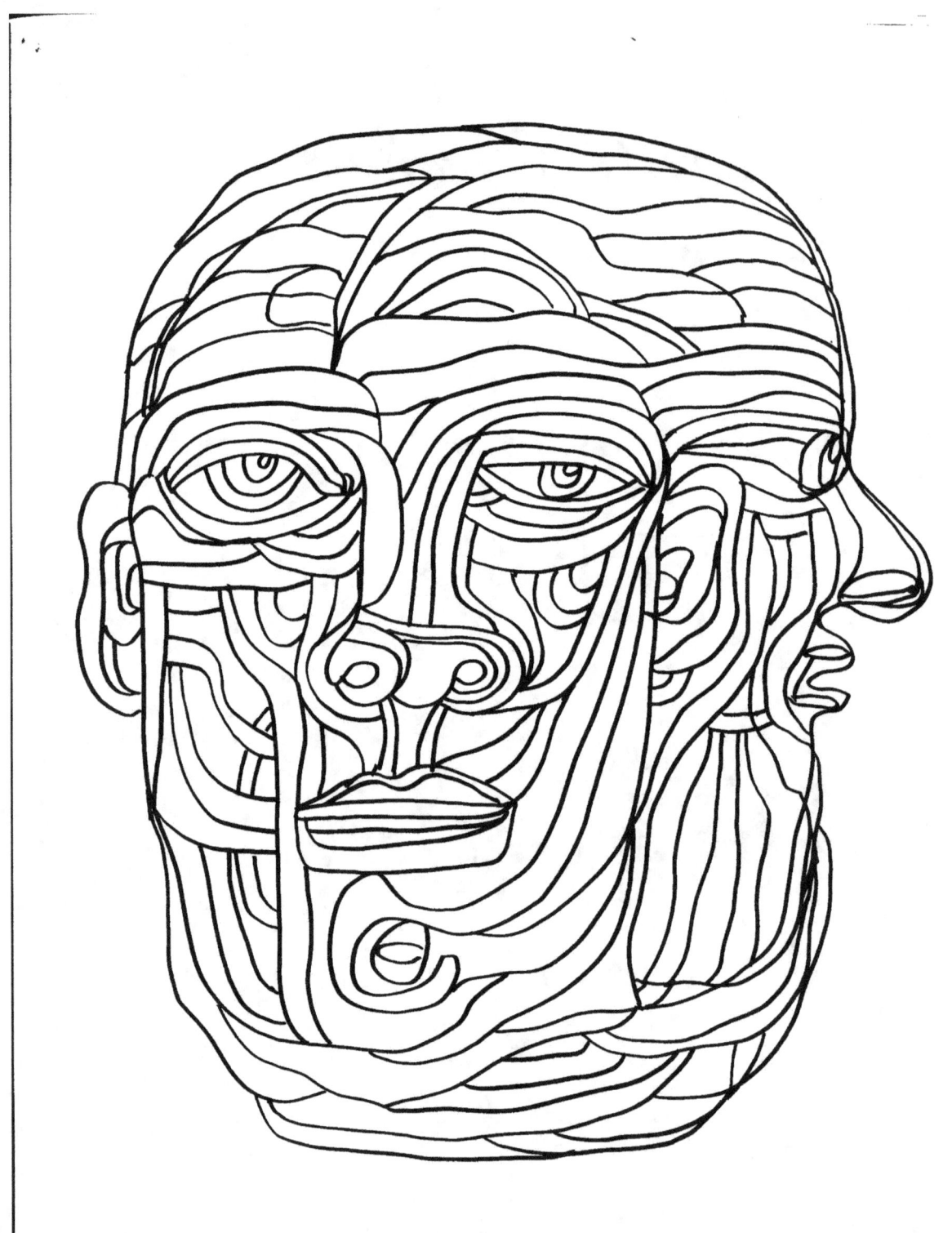

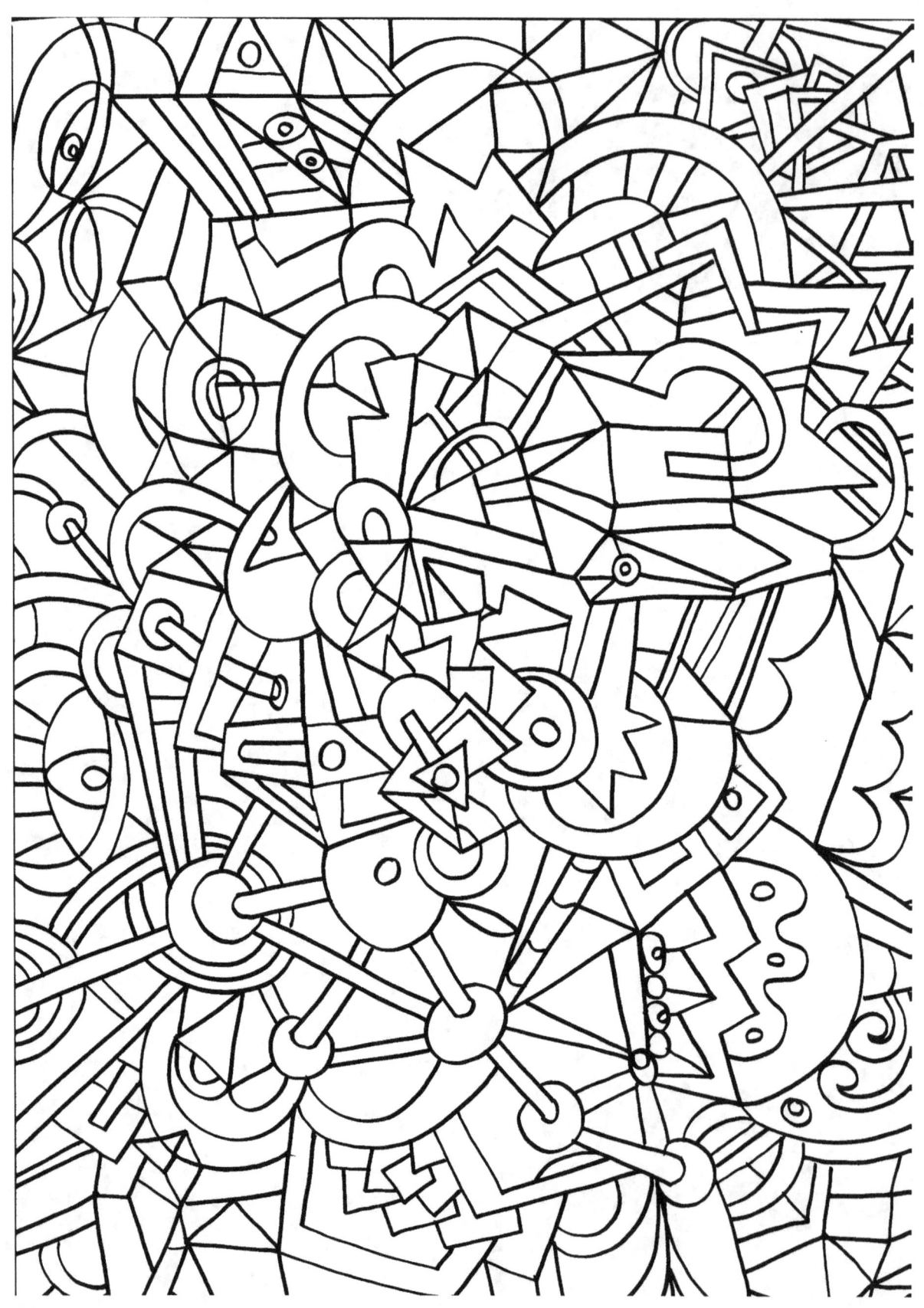

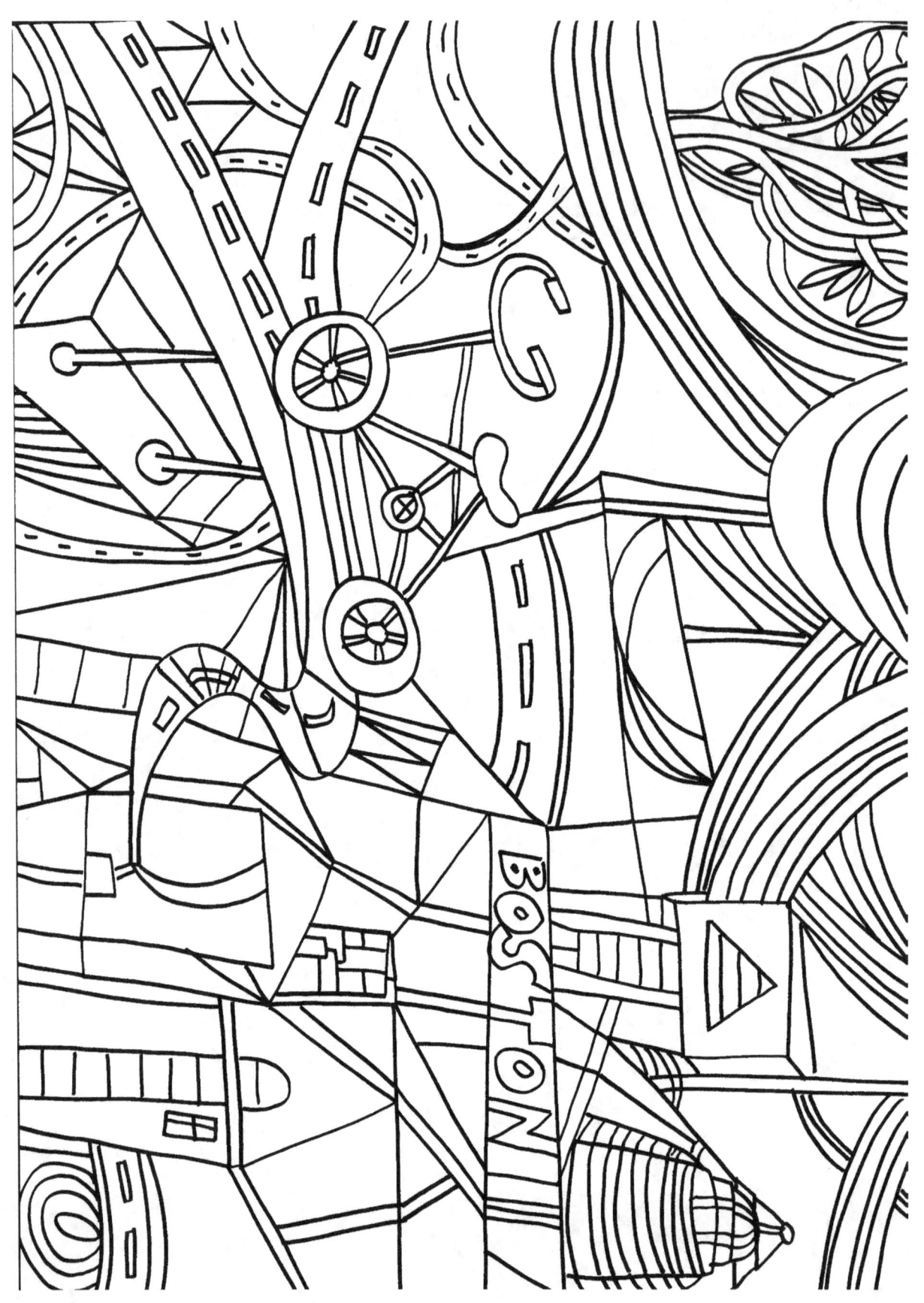

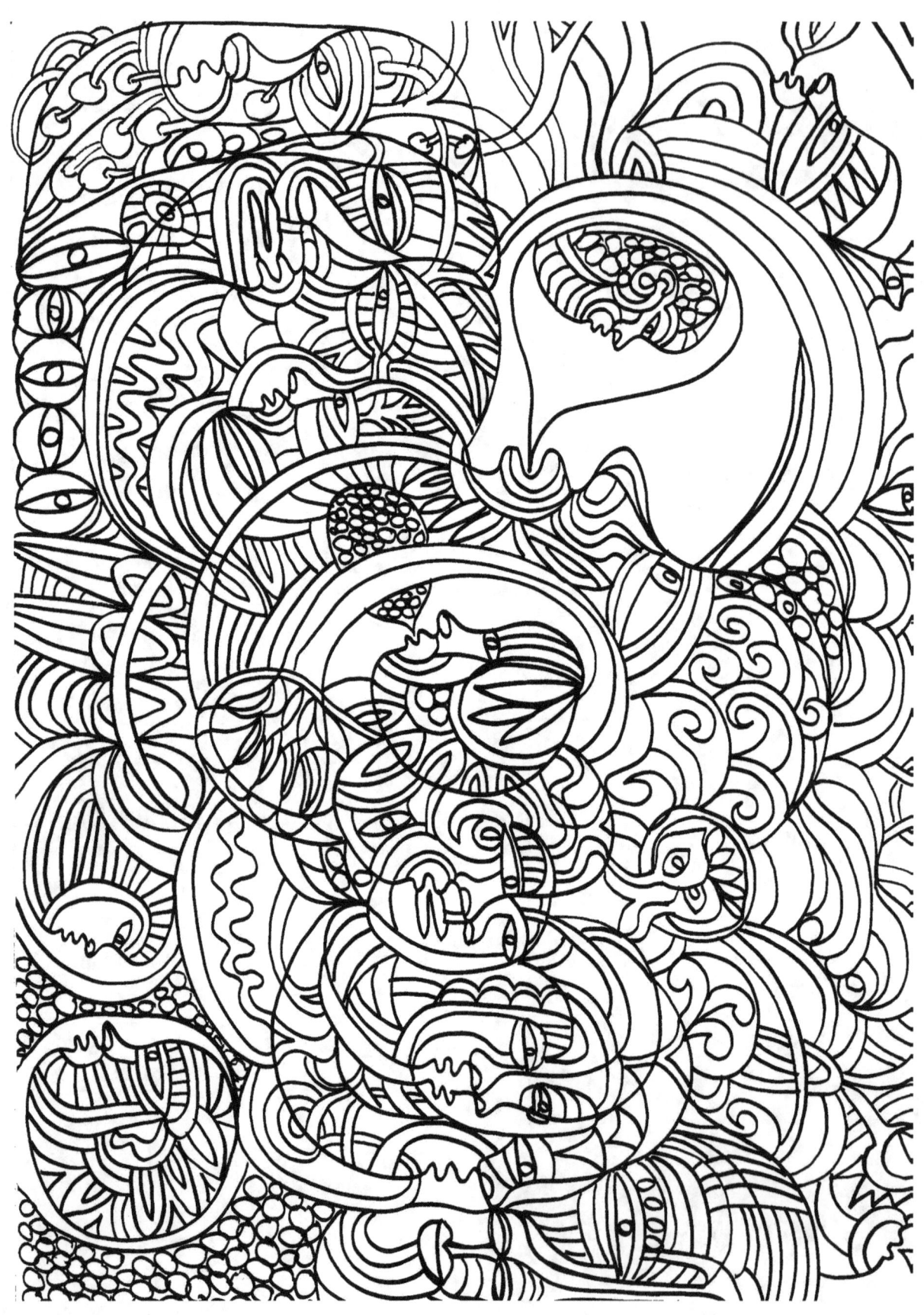

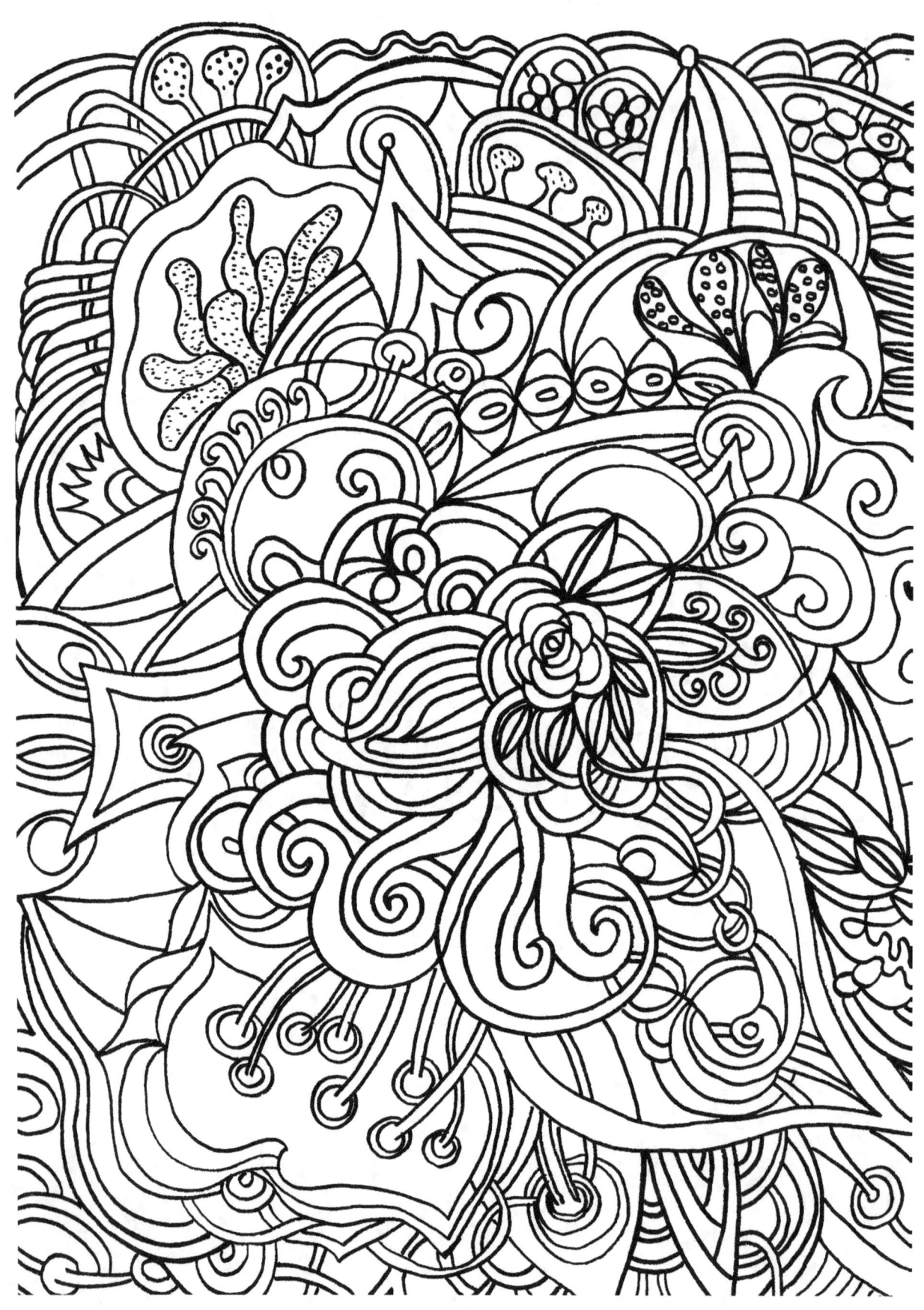

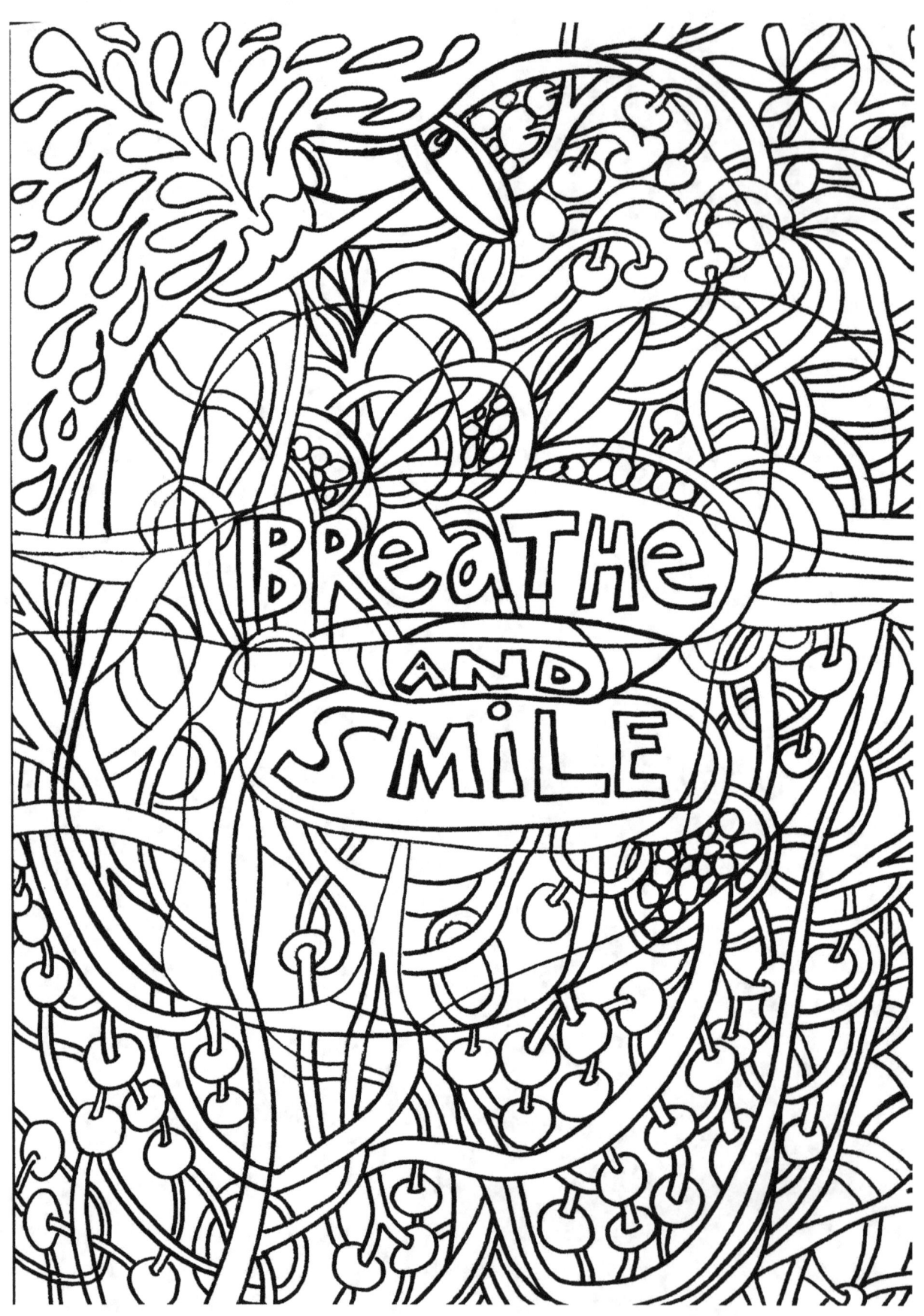

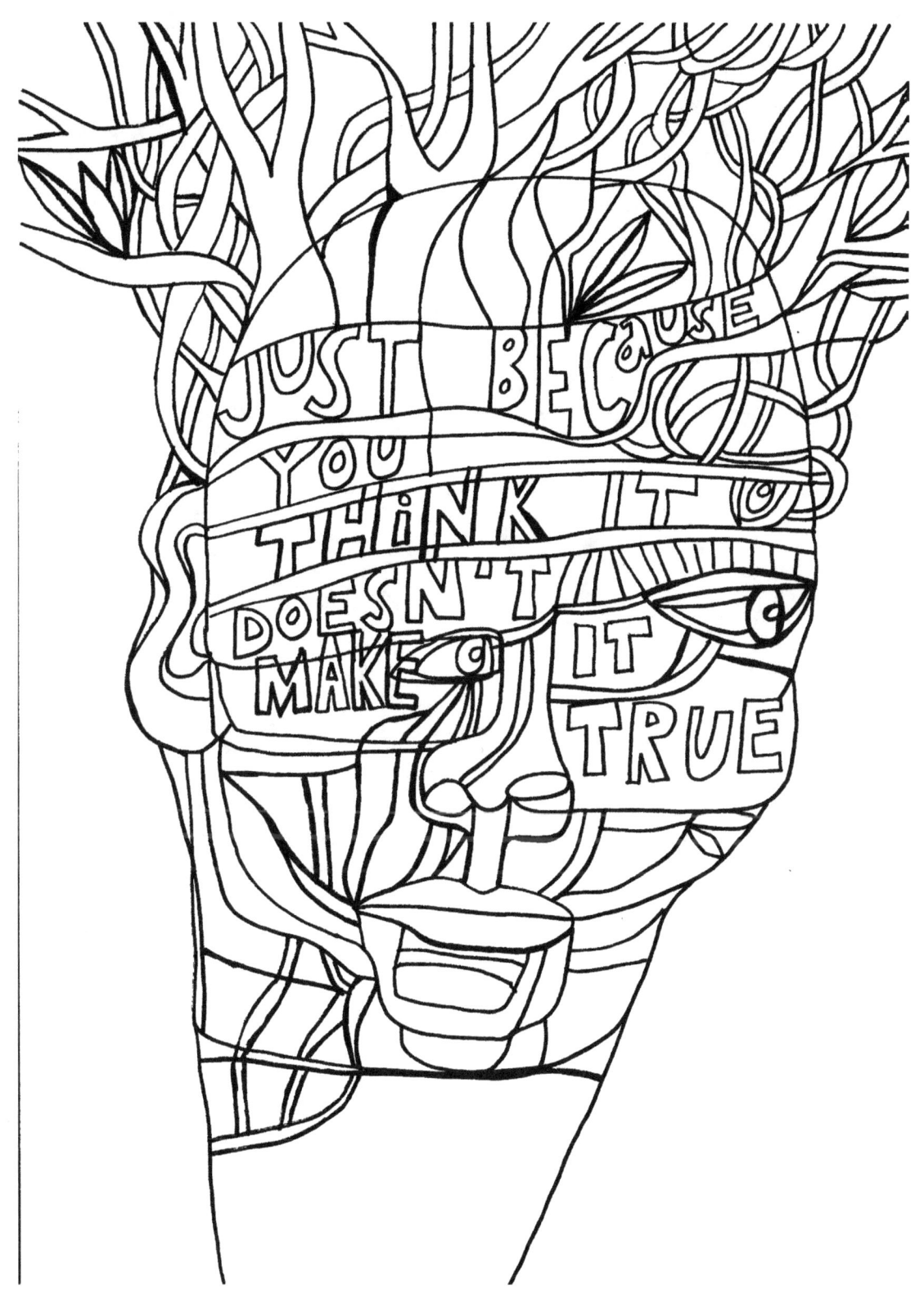

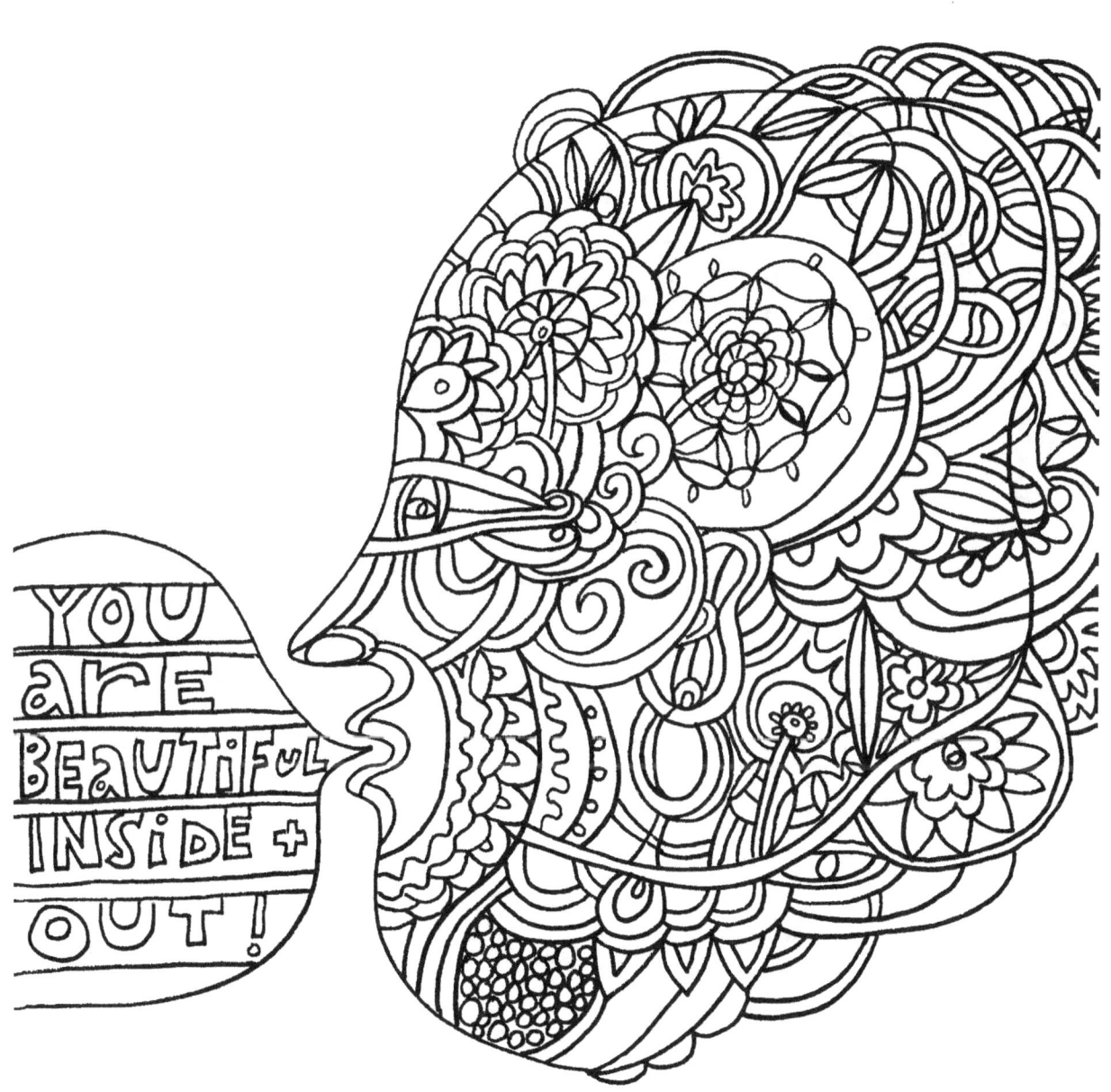

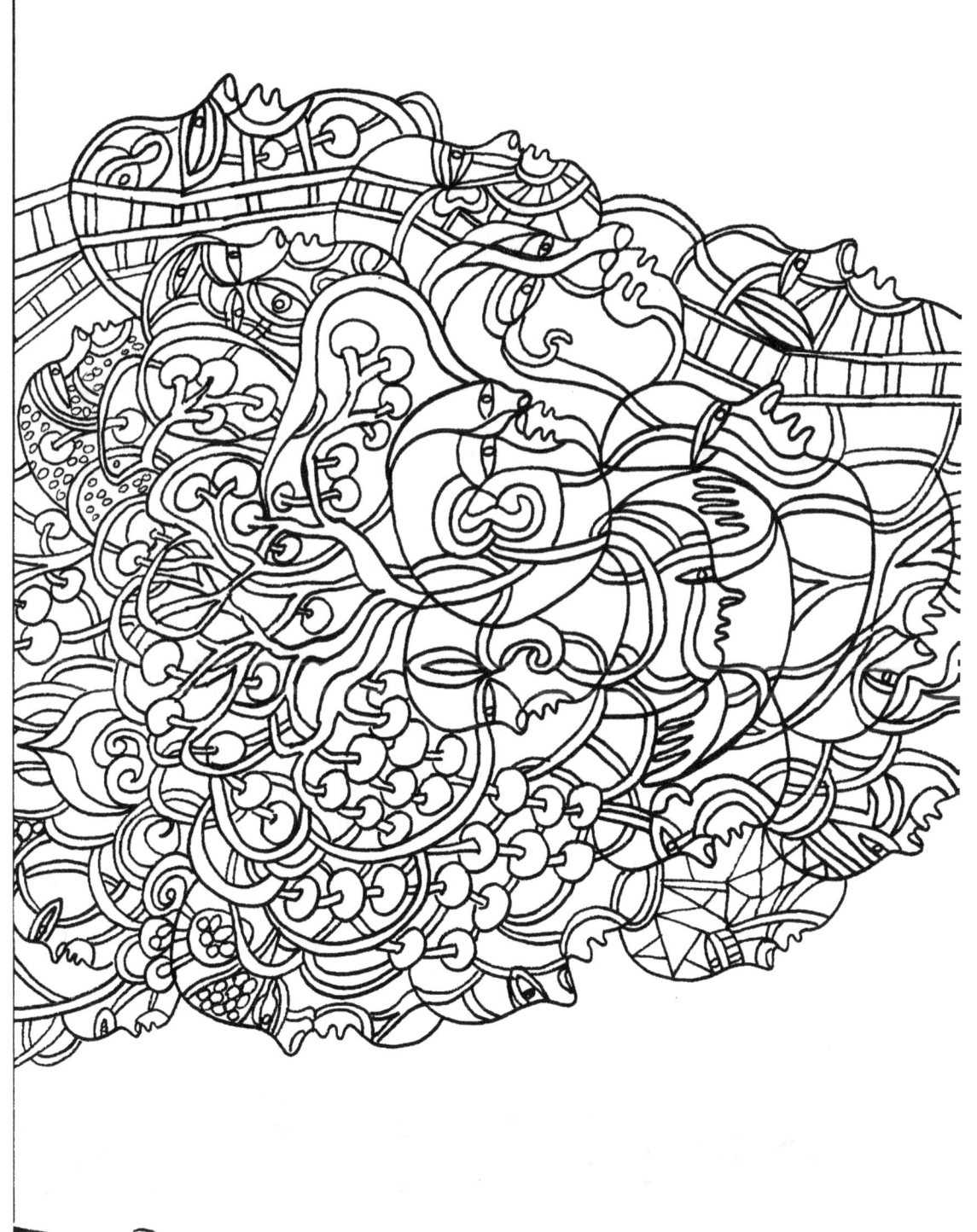

LET Your PENCIL DaNCE

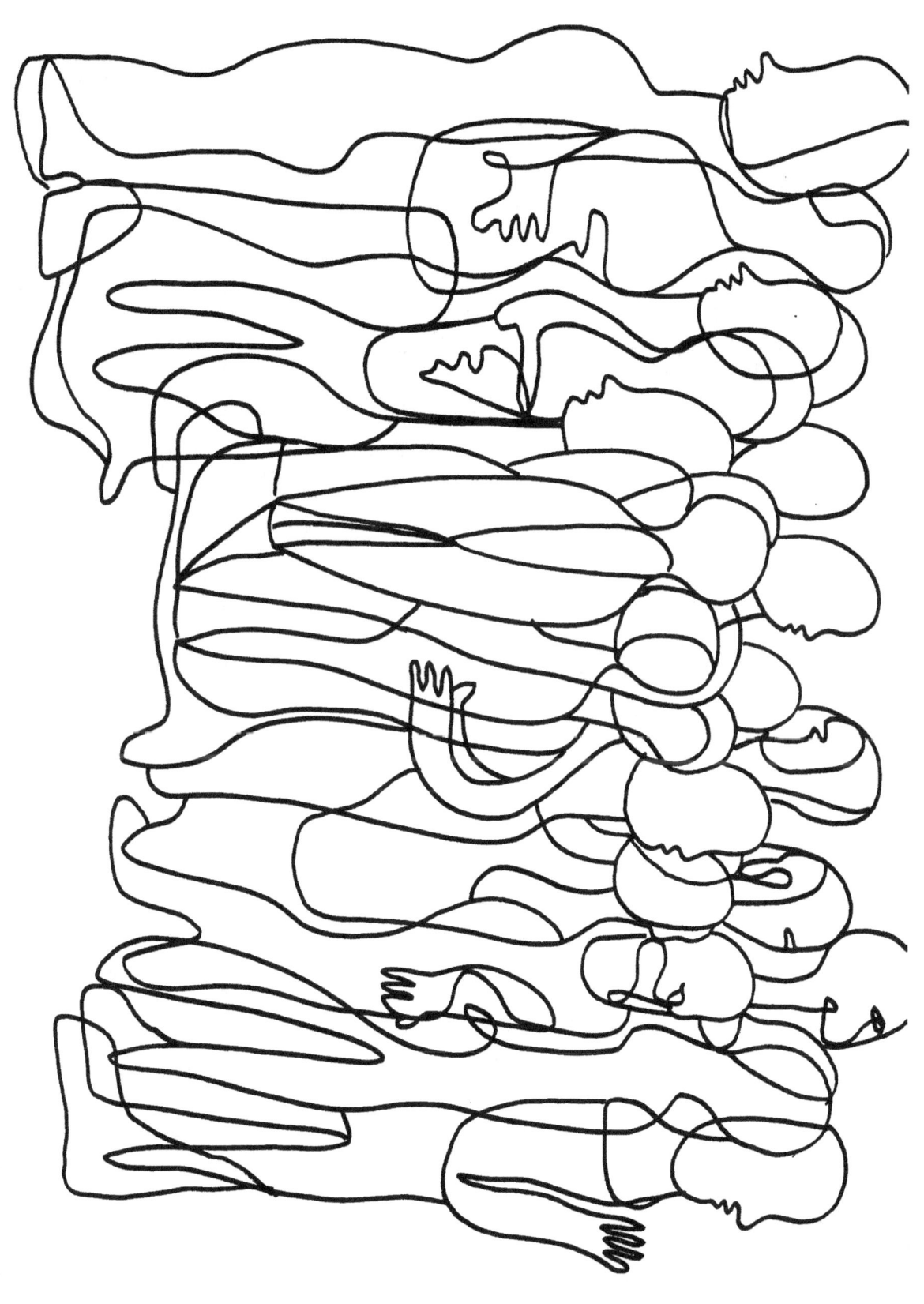

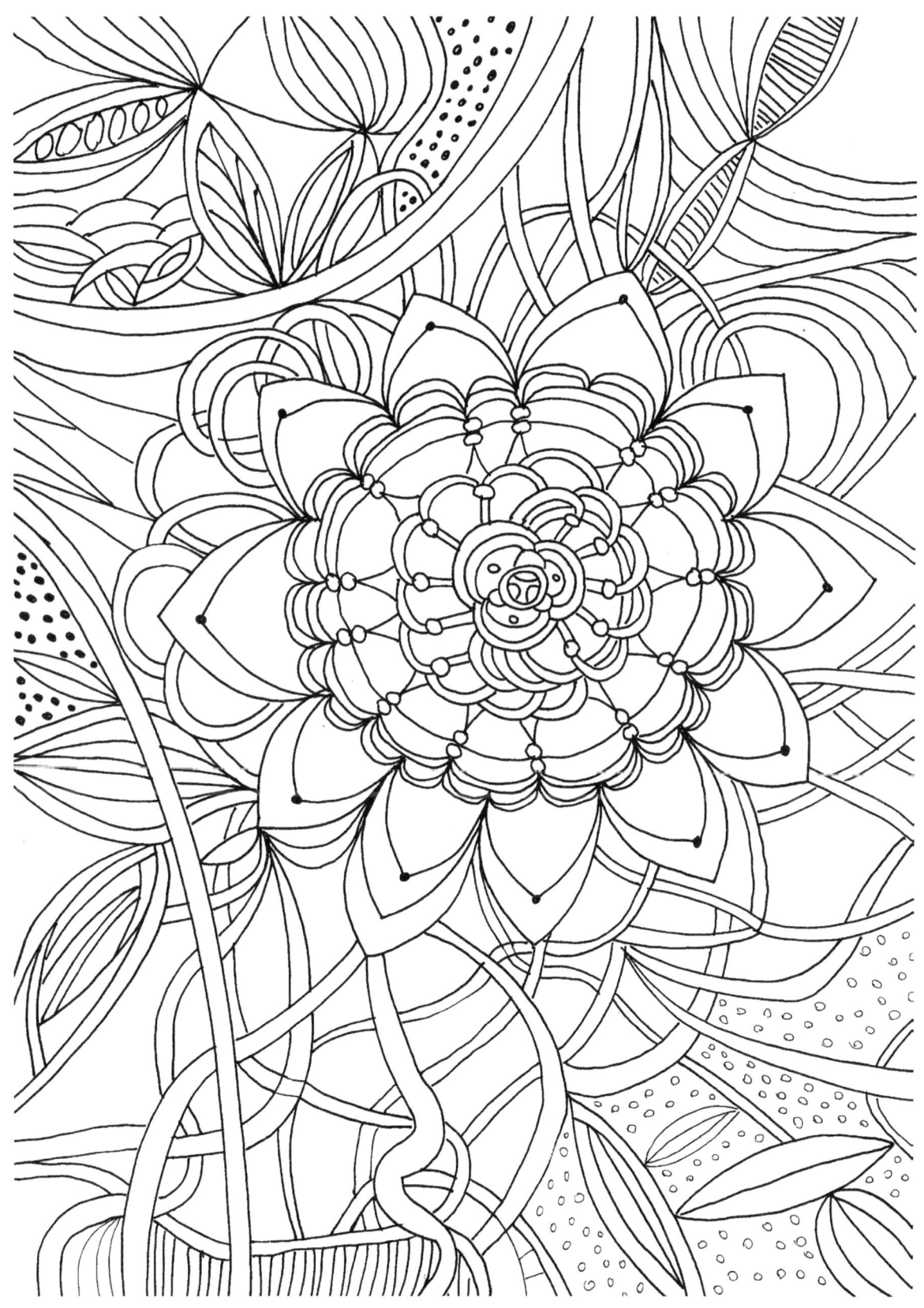

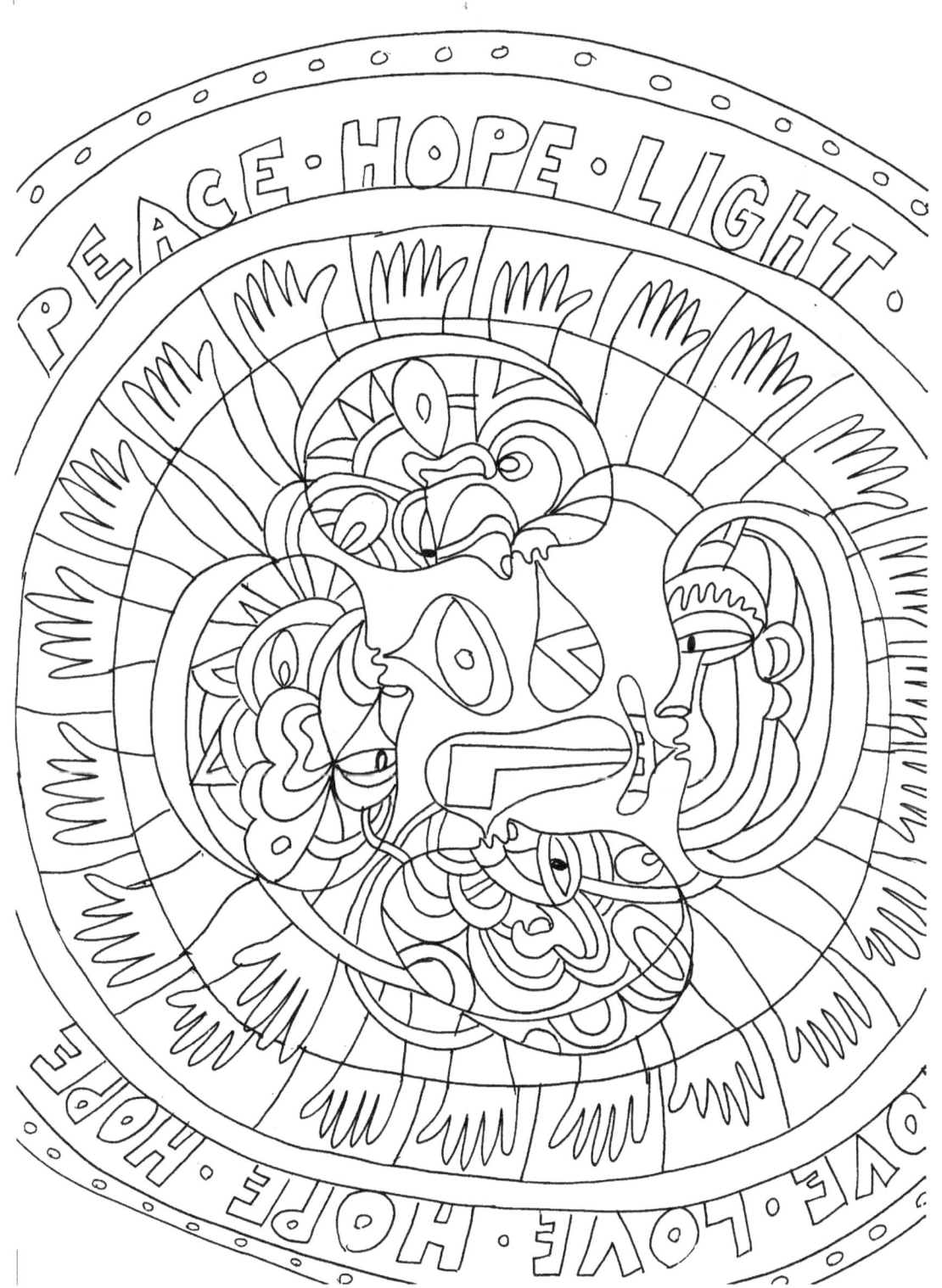

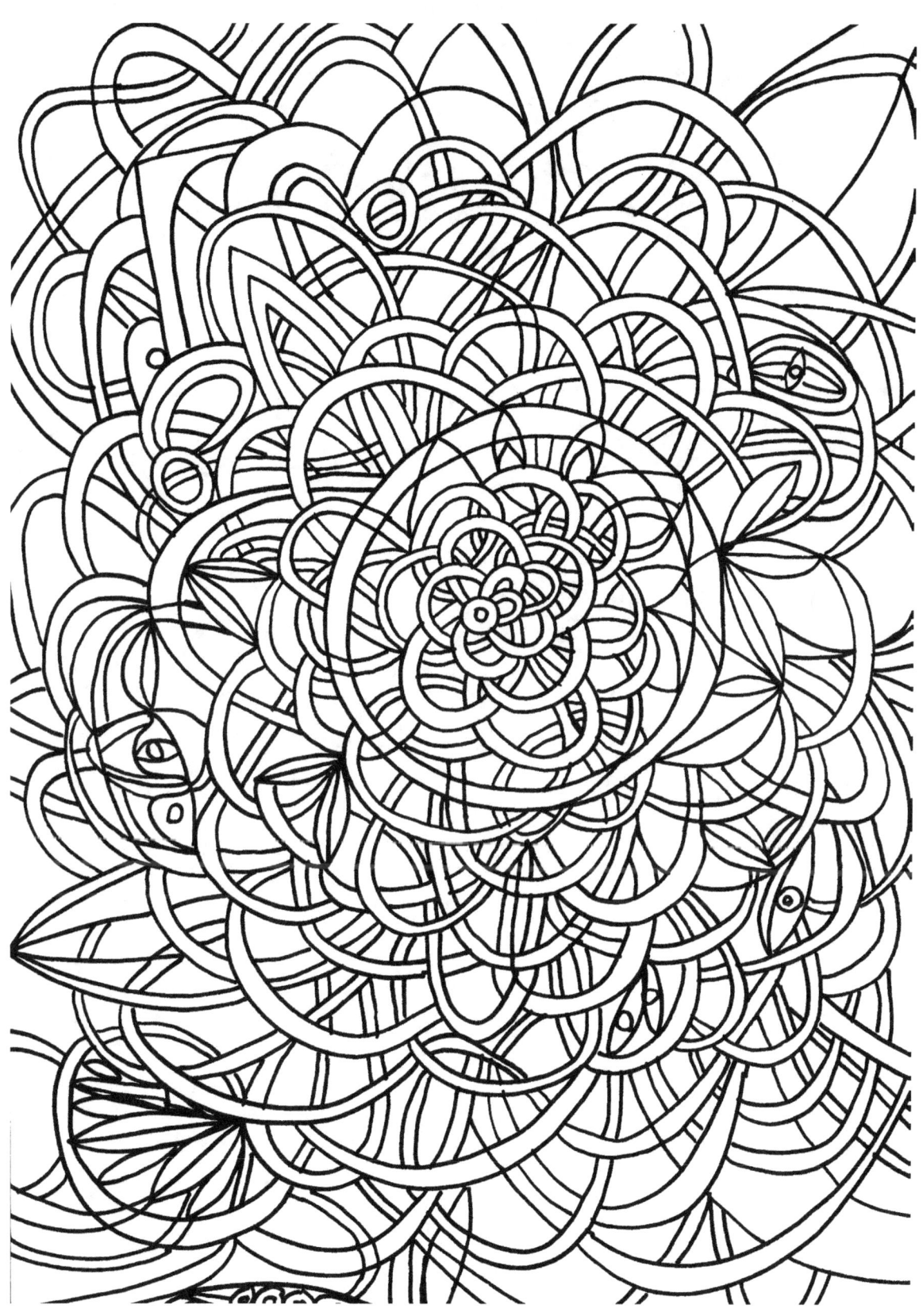

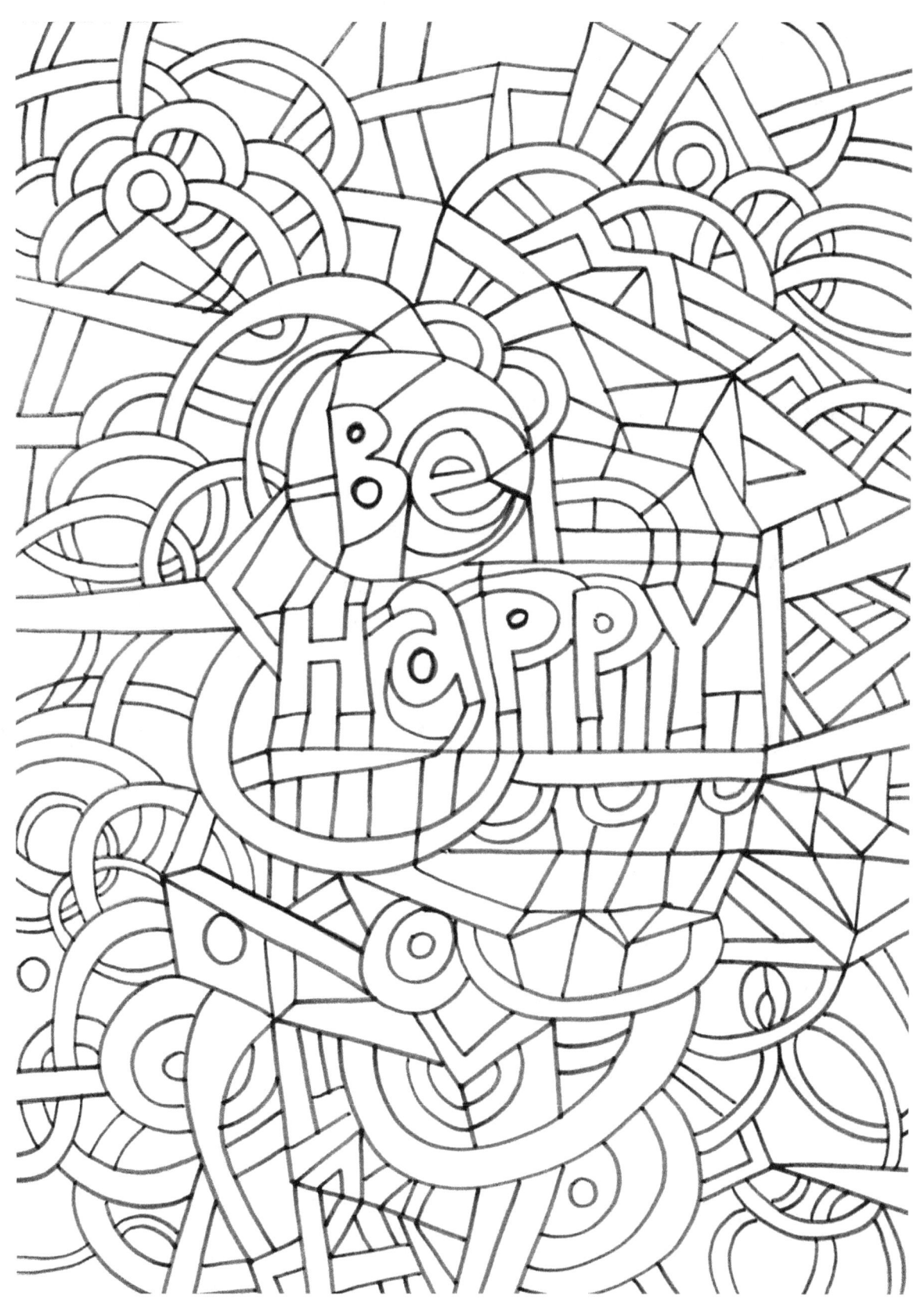

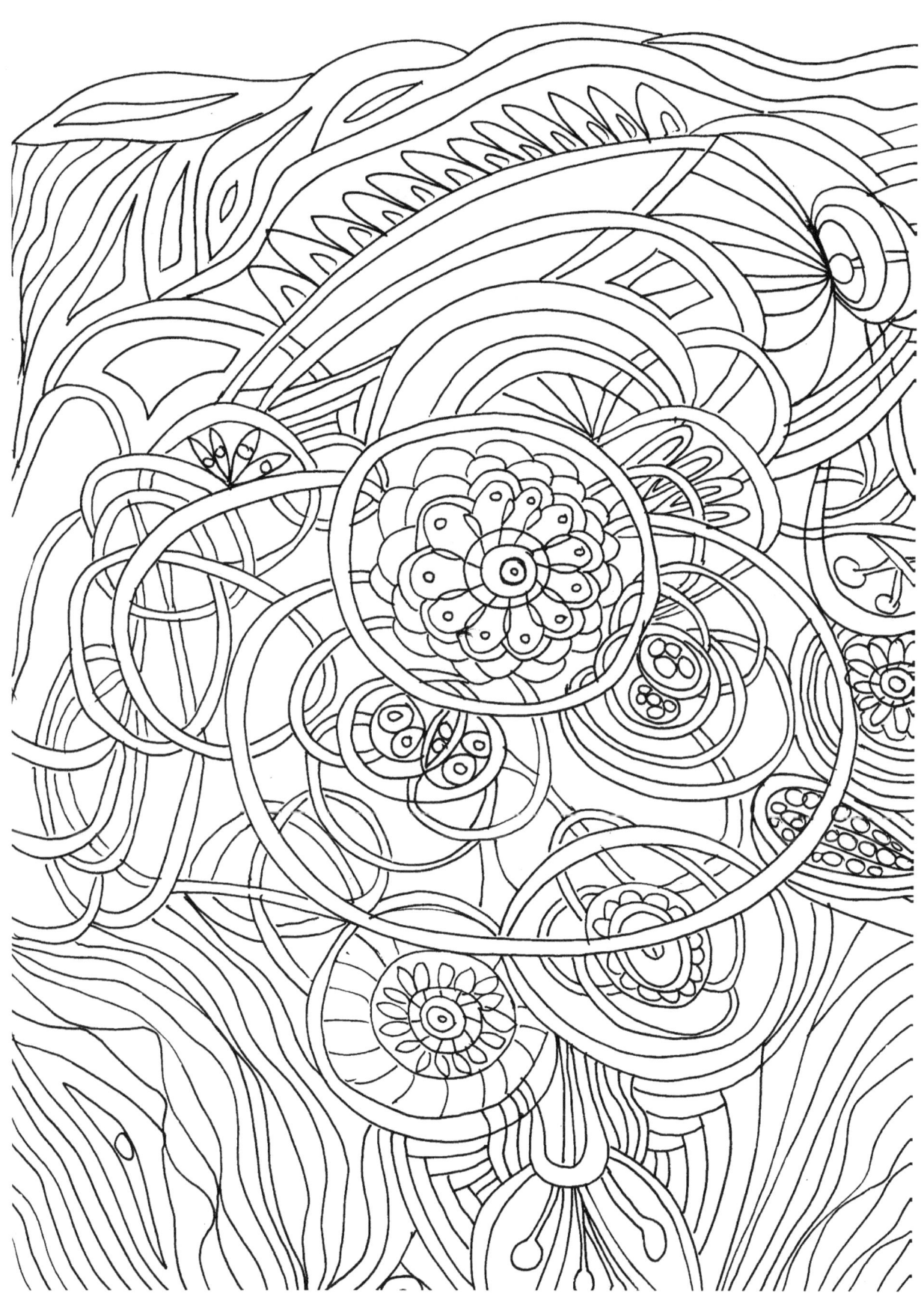

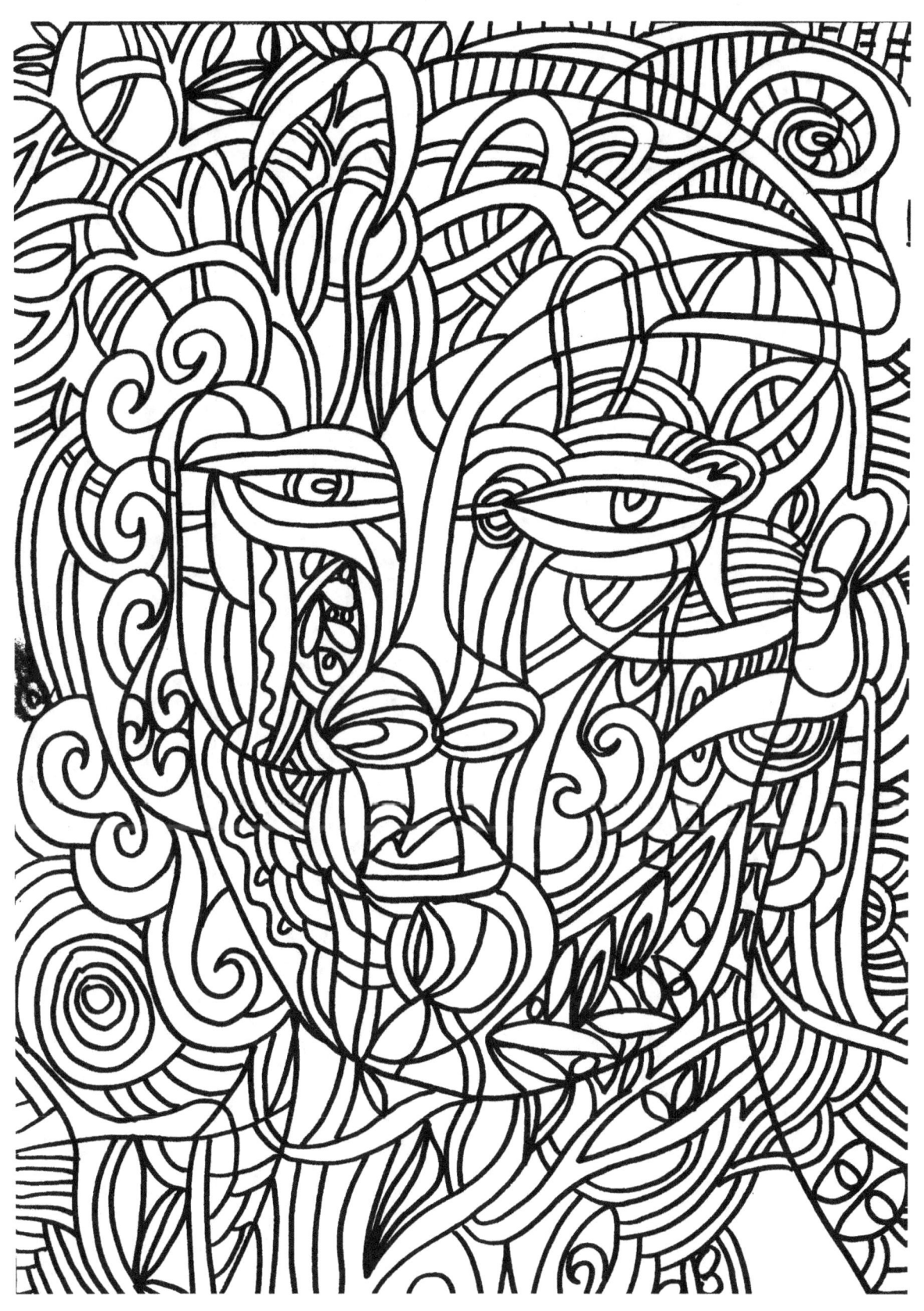

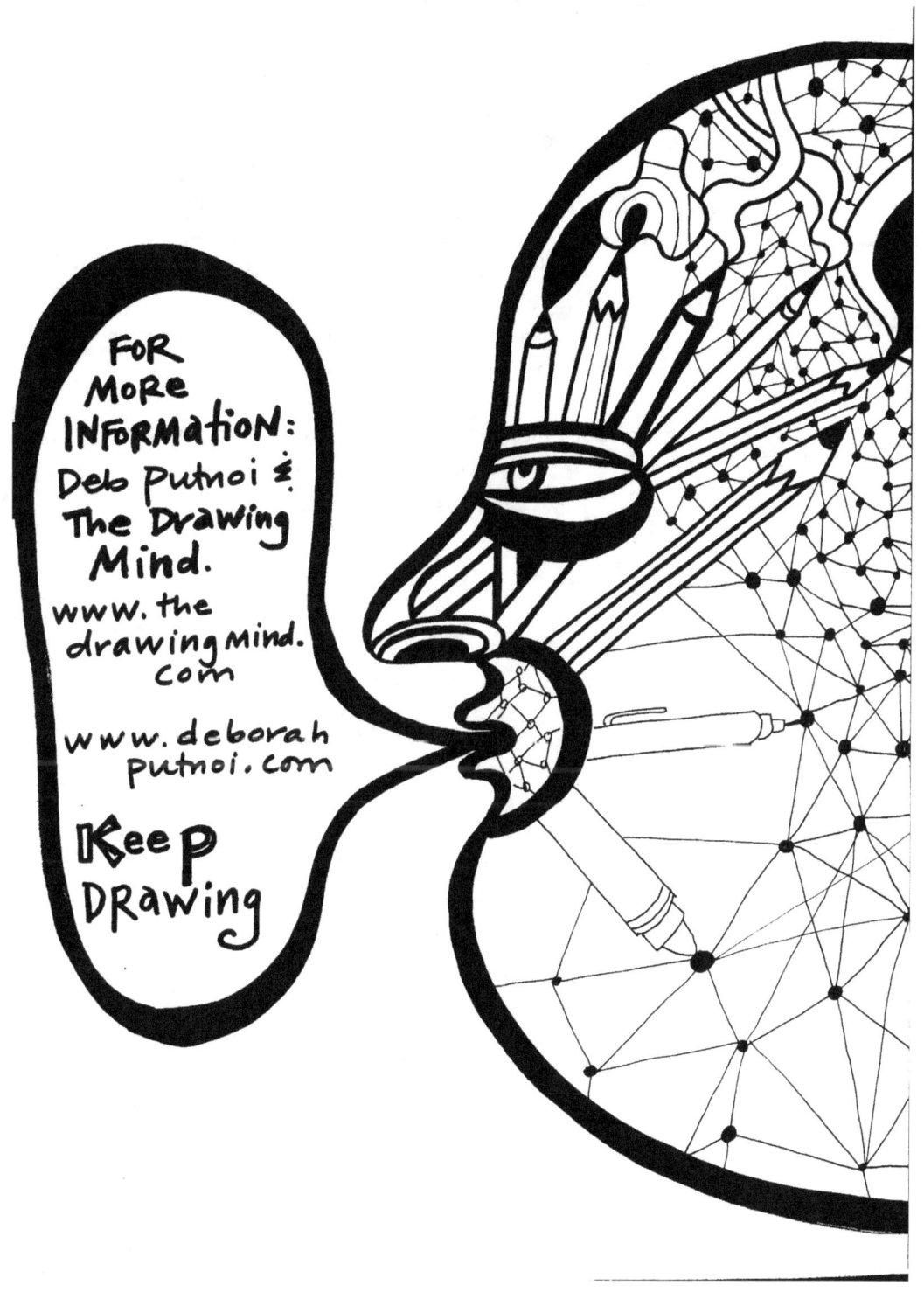

ABOUT THE AUTHOR

Deborah Putnoi is an artist and educator and
author of, "The Drawing Mind.
She graduated from Tufts University and
the School of the Museum of Fine Arts with a BA/BFA and
holds an MEd from the Harvard Graduate School of Education.
She lives in the Boston area with her two children,
her husband and their dog Coco.

To learn more about Deb and her art visit her at:
www.deborahputnoi.com

To learn more about The Drawing Mind and
The Drawing Lab visit:
www.thedrawingmind.com

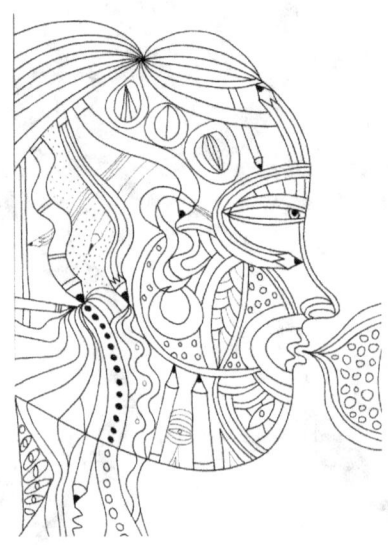